# BEER
## MEMORABILIA

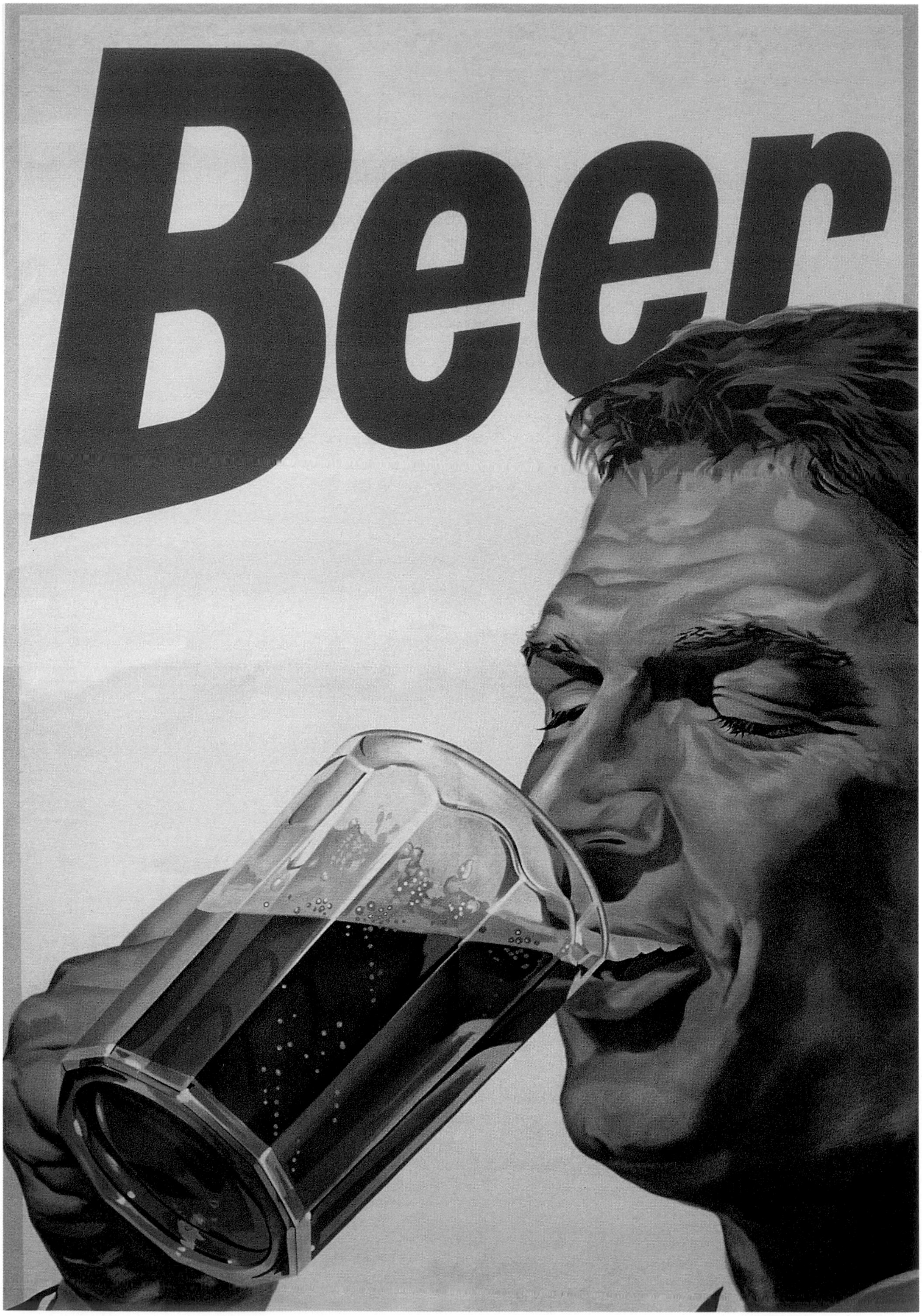
Beer

MARTYN CORNELL'S

# BEER
# MEMORABILIA

Collecting the best from around the world

**WITH THE NATIONAL ASSOCIATION
BREWERIANA ADVERTISING**

CHARTWELL
BOOKS, INC.

A QUINTET BOOK

Published by Chartwell Books
A Division of Book Sales, Inc.
114, Northfield Avenue, Edison, New Jersey 08837

This edition produced for sale in the USA,
its territories and dependencies only.

ISBN 0-7858-0940-6

This book was designed and produced by
Quintet Publishing Limited, 6 Blundell Street, London N7 9BH

Creative Director: Richard Dewing
Art Director: Simon Daley
Designer: James Lawrence
Senior Editor: Sally Green
Editor: Rosie Hankin

Typeset in Great Britain by
Central Southern Typesetters, Eastbourne
Manufactured in Hong Kong by Regent Publishing Services Ltd
Printed in Singapore by Star Standard Industries (Pte) Ltd

ACKNOWLEDGMENTS

Grateful thanks are due to the National Association Breweriana Advertising for the loan of material, and
also to the following individuals and organisations, for their invaluable help and contributions to this book:
Bill Austin, Nina and John Birkelund, Alan Bowers, Brasserie Cantillion, Carlsberg, Tom Coppack, Peter Gorman,
Holsten, Martin Kemp, Radoslav Kwiecien, Johan Lefever, John Law, Rostislav Lozovuk, Hugh Madgin, Neil Morgan,
The Frank J Mrazik Collection, Musée Européen de la Bière, Musée Français de la Brasserie, Jørgen Olsen, CA Pelton,
Bo Peterssen, Yuri V Pozdnyakov, Shao Hong Jiang, John Smith's Brewery, Enrique Solaesa, Dieter Treytnar,
Algimantas Venskevicius and most especially Emer O'Neill, for all her support.

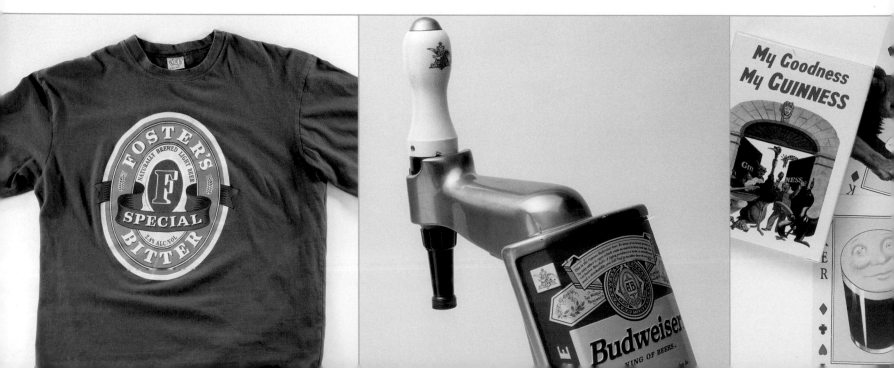

# Contents

# How beer is brewed

BEFORE SETTING OUT on the collecting trail, you should know what all the fuss is about. It's about beer. So let's have a look at how it is brewed. Brewing beer is, technically, much more complicated than making wine. Beer is made from grain, traditionally barley. The seeds of grain are soaked, which encourages them to start sprouting. As they sprout, enzymes in the grain turn the starch inside into sugar. At just the right moment the grain is heated in a kiln so that sprouting is stopped before all the sugar is used up by the growing seed. It is now known as malt.

The brewer takes the malt, grinds it coarsely, and adds hot water at a temperature that will encourage the remaining enzymes to convert the last of the starch to sugar – a process known as mashing. After a couple of hours in the mash tun (cask), now a sweet, sugary solution known as wort, is run off. Hops, the green cones of the female hop plant, are then added to the wort, which is boiled in a 'copper' to extract the bittering compounds from the hops.

The next stage is to cool the wort, run it into the fermenting vessels, and add yeast, a single-cell organism. The yeast 'eats' sugar in a process known as fermentation and, as a by-product, produces alcohol. When the yeast has done its work and turned the sugar into alcohol, the wort has become beer. It is bottled, canned, or put into casks and shipped out to the public.

For thousands of years ancient brewers would add flavorings, using such plants as bog myrtle, ground ivy, and herb bennet. Eventually it was discovered that one flavoring, the hop plant, not only gave a pleasant bitter taste to the drink but also helped it keep much longer before it went sour. In England the hop-flavored drink was introduced by brewers from The Netherlands and Flanders, who called it *bier,* and for a couple of centuries unhopped ale and hopped beer existed alongside each other in Britain, until finally even the ale brewers began using hops as well.

Brewers have known for a long time that if you store beer it will often improve in flavor. The German for 'store' is *lager*, and thus stored beer is called *lager bier* in Germany. It was believed that a particular type of yeast takes over at cold temperatures. It sits at the bottom of the fermenting vessel rather than at the top, as yeast that prefers warmer temperatures does. The Latin name for the yeast that makes beer is *Saccharomyces cerevisiae*. For many years the bottom-fermenting type used for making lager was thought to be a different breed, and it was called *Saccharomyces carlsbergiensis*, named for the Carlsberg brewery in Denmark where it was first recognized and isolated. Today, however, DNA studies have shown that lager yeast is the same organism as ordinary beer yeast.

Left **Checking the temperature of the mash at the Cantillon brewery, Anderlecht, Brussels, Belgium, where much of the equipment dates from its foundation in 1900.**

Above **Adding hops to the copper at the Cantillon brewery, Anderlecht.**

Above right **Hops give a pleasant bitter taste and have a preservative quality.**

# A short history of beer

THE ROOTS OF THE STORY OF BEER are in the Middle East, in the crescent of land that stretches from northern Israel through Lebanon and western Syria to southeastern Turkey and northern Iraq. There, on the hilly flanks of the mountain regions, the wild ancestors of today's barley and wheat still grow. Around 10,000 years ago the local people began the first steps in cultivating these plants, rather than simply gathering the grain where it sprang up on the hillsides.

At first the early farmers ate the grains as porridge or gruel, with bread probably invented centuries later. Eventually, from bread came beer. The earliest brewing techniques we know about, from Sumer, in the Middle East, and ancient Egypt, involved soaking bread in water and letting wild yeasts ferment the liquid into beer. A similar bread-beer was still made in modern times by home brewers in eastern Finland, where it was called *taari*.

We do not know when beer was invented; archeologists are still arguing. It was probably after the invention of pottery, which appeared in the Middle East around 8,500 years ago. The first clear clue of the start of beer drinking is found on a 6,000-year-old seal used for stamping designs on wet clay, discovered at a place called Tepe Gawra, northwest of Nineveh in Mesopotamia (modern Iraq). The stamp shows two figures drinking through straws out of a large pot, just the way beer was consumed later in the Middle East. The first 'solid' – literally – evidence is three or four centuries later, however. Pottery from the late fourth millennium BC, around 5,500 years ago, found at Godin Tepe, a Sumerian outpost in the Zagros mountains of Iran, shows traces of calcium oxalate. This is 'beer stone,' a natural deposit in beer. The jars had grooves inside, which may have been designed to trap yeast, which would have helped to start the next brew when fresh ingredients were subsequently added.

## Drinking beer with golden straws

Around 1,600 years later in Sumer proper (modern southern Iraq), beer lovers in the ancient city of Ur were still drinking their beer through straws. Gold drinking straws were found in the tomb of a Sumerian noblewoman called Pu-abi, and a banquet scene depicted on a cylinder-shaped seal found in the same tomb shows a male and female seated on either side of a wide-mouthed jar sucking up beer through drinking tubes. The use of straws may be because early Middle Eastern beer was not strained so still had grain husks and the like floating in it, or perhaps it was simply because drinking through straws is fun. The Greek general and historian Xenophon found Armenian villagers

drinking beer through straws in 400BC, and there are reports of Norwegian farmers drinking their home-brewed beer through straws in the nineteenth century.

The general Sumerian word for beer was *kas*, and there were several different kinds: *kas-gig*, for example, was dark beer, and *kas-kal* was strong beer. The early Sumerian pictogram sign for beer looks like a grooved jar of the type apparently used for brewing. The Sumerians had a goddess of beer, whom they gave the name Ninkasi, and about 3,800 years ago someone composed a poem in her praise. It was a popular enough work for some copies in Sumerian cuneiform script to have survived. They were found by modern archeologists in the ruins of three different ancient Sumerian cities. When the 'Hymn to Ninkasi' was translated, it was found to be a recipe, in effect, for making Sumerian bread-beer. By this time the brew included malted grain, as well as bread, while the Sumerians evidently added dates and/or honey as well, to give flavor and extra fermentable sugars to the beer. The recipe was accurate enough for a modern brewer, Fritz Maytag of the Anchor brewery in San Francisco, together with Solomon Katz, an American archeologist, to attempt to re-create Ninkasi's beer. The result was a pleasing dry, ciderlike drink with an alcohol content of around 4.4 percent by volume.

In Egypt beer brewing was taking place in the predynastic period, more than 5,000 years ago. Beer residues have been found at the bottom of pottery jars that have been made at that time. The ancient Egyptian word for beer was *henket*, or to be more exact *hnkt*. (The

**Below Advertising during World War II by C Schmidt & Sons' brewery in Philadelphia, showing ancient beer drinking scenes.**

Left **A medieval tavern of the fourteenth century**

Egyptian writing system consisted purely of consonants, and we can only guess at what vowels were used.) Beer, along with bread, onions, and beans, was one of the staples of the Egyptian diet. Like Sumerian beer, early Egyptian beer was made from bread soaked in water and allowed to ferment. It was so important that models of brewers making a batch of beer, with loaves being soaked in two-foot-high jars, were left in tombs to 'supply' beer to the dead.

## Female brewers in Ancient Egypt

By the time of the so-called New Kingdom in Egypt, between 3,550 and 3,100 years ago (the period best known for the pharaoh Tutankhamun), Egyptian brewers were using malted grain, both barley and a type of husked wheat called emmer. Beer brewing was done by the women, who looked after the fermentation and filtered the finished beer. They may also have added extra sugar in the form of dates and/or honey, to make a stronger drink.

The favorite brew in northern Europe, meanwhile, was mead, which is fermented honey and water. Mead was certainly drunk by the Beaker Folk, whose name comes from the pottery drinking vessels that were buried with them in their graves. They arrived in Britain about 3,800 years ago, and their beakers show a remarkable similarity to pottery beer mugs. One Bronze Age beaker found in a grave in Fife, Scotland, showed traces of mead made from honey from the north of England, flavored with meadowsweet, a fragrant flower found in meadows and by streams. Another beaker was found in a Bronze Age burial place of a young woman in Strathallen, just north of Gleneagles, in Tayside, Scotland. Pollen analysis revealed it had held a cereal-based drink again

flavored with meadowsweet, perhaps a bread-based honey-beer halfway between beer and mead. (The meadowsweet has another role besides flavoring: tests have shown that using it in a brew extends the shelf-life of a hop-free bread-beer by several weeks.)

Mead was also the favourite drink among the Celts, the people who followed the Beaker Folk to Britain. Honey was the earliest sweetener, and mead was probably the first alcoholic drink known to all the Indo-European peoples, who include not only the Celts, but the Germans, Slavs, Italians, Greeks, and Indo-Iranians. We know this because of the range of words from the same root – cover the meanings mead, honey, sweet, and drunk or intoxicated – found in Indo-European languages from Ireland to India. In Welsh, for example, *mêl* is honey, *medd* is mead, and *meddw* is drunk; while 'drunk' in Greek was *methúskein*. In Hindi, *mádhu* means honey or sweetness, and *mádati* in Sanskrit, the ancient language of India, means gets drunk.

## Beer from berries and bees

However mead was expensive so in the Bronze Age, northern Europeans would mix honey with malted wheat, and even berries to make a kind of honey-fruit-beer. A birch-bark container found in a Bronze Age burial site in Denmark contained traces of just such a drink, which included honey, wheat (probably emmer, the same wheat used for brewing by the Egyptians), and cranberries. It was flavored with sweet gale, otherwise known as bog myrtle, a plant that was put into ale right through to medieval times, and which is still used now to flavor Danish brandy. Honey-beers are occasionally made today: one is Waggle Dance, named for the 'dance' a bee makes on its return to the hive to tell its fellow bees the direction to go, in order to find the best nectar-bearing flowers. It is brewed by Vaux of Sunderland, in the northeast of England.

A burial site dating from 800BC, 2,800 years ago, was found near the modern village of Kasendorf, in northern Bavaria, then occupied by Celtic tribes. It contained crocks that had once held beer made from bread. But honey-beer continued to be preferred by the Celts. Around 320BC the Greek explorer Pytheas came to Britain and found the local Celts busy making beer from wheat and honey. Their continental cousins did the same. Another Greek, Poseidonius, writing about the drinking habits of the Celts of southern Gaul (the Provence area of modern France) in the early first century BC, said that while the wealthy drank imported wine, 'among the needier inhabitants a beer is drunk made from wheat with honey added ... called corma.'

The wheat for this mixed drink was still emmer, which was known to the Celts as *bracis*. From this word came the name of the honey-and-grain drink in Old Welsh, *bragaut*, which became *bragget* in English. Bragget (honey beer) was brewed until the seventeenth century, and

Chaucer talks about it in the *The Canterbury Tales*, saying of Alisoun, the carpenter's wife in *The Miller's Tale*, that 'hire mouth was sweete as braket or the meth' (meth, of course, being mead). *Bracis* is also the root of the French words for brewer, *brasseur*, and brewery, *brasserie*. In English a brasserie now means a restaurant serving simple, uncomplicated food, from the habit of eating in a brewery garden.

The Roman writer Pliny, who lived from AD23 to 79, wrote in his *Natural History* that the 'nations of the west' have their own intoxicant *'made from grain boiled with water; there are a number of ways of making it in Gaul and Spain, under different names, although the principle is the same. The Spanish provinces have even taught us that these [liquors] will bear being kept for a long time.'* Pliny gives the names of the different brews as *caelia* and *cerea* in Spain, and *cervesia* 'and several other kinds' in Gaul. Pliny also mentions hops, though only as a 'delicacy' for eating, not as a flavoring for ale. Dioscorides, a Greek living in Asia Minor in the first century AD, wrote in a book called *De Medica Materia*, of 'curmi, made of barley... there are like sorts of drink made from wheat in "Iberia Occidentalis" (western Spain) and Britain.'

## Beer becomes the workers' drink

After the Romans subjugated the Celts first in Gaul and then, from AD43, in Britain, ale brewing never stopped. In Britain, Roman central heating technology (the hypocaust) was adapted to build better maltings to make malt for brewing. While the well-off in Roman Britain drank wine, the drink of the ordinary people was ale. In Verulamium (now St Albans in Hertfordshire), for example, a cook shop with attached brewery stood opposite the public baths for three centuries. Further north, on the border of Roman Britain and the Pictish lands of

Above **An early advertisement for Irish porter, dated 1780. Sweetman's stopped brewing in 1895.**

modern Scotland, the soldiers drank ale, as they doubtless did elsewhere in Britain. A series of domestic and military accounts written on wooden tablets found at the Roman fort of Vindolanda in modern Northumbria, dating to around AD110, mention 'Atrectus the brewer' (the first named brewer in British history), and also purchases of ale, and emmer for malting.

Ale was drunk at this time in Ireland as well. The Irish epic poem *The Cattle Raid of Cooley* describes a day in the life of King Conor Mac Nessa, who ruled over Ulster around the end of the first century AD,

Far left **Landlord and drinkers at a seventeenth-century inn.**

Left **A German brewhouse in 1568, showing the mash tun (in the background) being stirred, the cooler (at the top), the fermenting vessels, and the barrels being filled with beer.**

that would be the envy of any couch potato today. In a voice that makes it clear this is the way all kings should behave, the poet says that when Conor was at his great palace near Armagh, he would spend a third of the day watching the youths at sport (the ancient equivalent of watching football on the tube); a third playing 'fidchell,' a popular Iron Age board game; and the last third of the day drinking ale 'until he falls asleep therefrom.'

Soon after the arrival of the Romans in Britain the original Celtic word for ale, *corma* or *courmi*, began to be pronounced with a 'v' sound in place of the 'm' (in the same way that the old Celtic kingdom of Dumnonia became Devon), so that it became closer to *corva*. From this Celtic word came the Latin for beer, *cervisia* or *cervesia*. Latin then gave Spanish its word for beer, *cerveza*, while in Portuguese it became *cerveja*. In medieval Welsh the word was spelt *cwrwf* (a single 'f' is pronounced 'v' in Welsh), which has become *cwrw* in the modern language.

The German tribes, who were the Celts' neighbors in Europe were also lovers of beer. The Roman historian Tacitus, writing around AD98, said of the Germans that 'their drink is a liquor made from barley or other grain which is fermented to produce a certain resemblance to wine.' He suggested that the Romans should use the Germans' liking for beer to conquer them. 'If we wanted to make use of their addiction to drink, by giving them as much of it as they want, we could defeat them as easily by means of this vice as with our weapons.' In those areas of Germany that the Romans did conquer, several breweries have been found. One, for example, served the city of Castra Regina (modern Regensburg) on the banks of the Danube. The archeologists who dug it up in 1983 found evidence of a kiln and mash tun, showing Europe's early brewers had moved on from bread-beer to something modern brewers would recognize.

## Cervesia, camum, and zythum

Beer was important enough to be among the items listed by the Roman Emperor Diocletian when he issued an edict in AD301 setting out the permitted prices for different goods and services in the empire, in an (unsuccessful) attempt to curb price inflation. Three types of beer were included in the edict: *cervesia* and *camum*, to be sold at four denarii per 'Italian pint,' and *zythum*, Egyptian beer, to be sold at two denarii a pint. For comparison, the very best Falernian wine was priced at 30 denarii a pint, and ordinary wine, *vini rustici*, was eight denarii a pint. *Camum*, or *kamos*, was a type of beer found in Pannonia (modern Hungary) and other eastern parts of the empire. It appears to be the root of the old Dutch words *kamme* or *kam*, meaning brewery, and *kammen*, meaning to brew. When the Romans left Britain around AD410, the Angles and Saxons began to arrive and push the native British back to Wales and

Right **The gates from the former Vezelise brewery, France, now installed in front of the disused maltings at the beer museum in Stenay, France.**

Cornwall. The invaders from Germany brought their taste for beer with them. The Anglo-Saxon word for beer was *alu* (in Anglian) or *ealu* (in West Saxon). The same word is found across northern and eastern Europe, in Finnish (*olut*), Lithuanian (*alùs*), Estonian (*olu*), Swedish (*öl*), and Danish and Norwegian (*øl*). In modern English, of course, it became ale.

Old English contained many compound words using *ealu*, which together give a sketch of Anglo-Saxon drinking habits: *ealu-hus*, or alehouse; *ealu-benc*, or ale bench; *ealu-wósa*, 'ale-wetter' or ale drinker; *ealo-gál*, 'ale-drunk'; *ealu-scop*, 'ale-poet', one who recites poetry where there is drinking; *ealu-sceop*, brewer; *ealo-geweorc*, 'ale-working' or brewing; and *ealu-cleofa*, cell or chamber for storing ale. There was also the *ealu gafol*, the ale tax, or tribute paid in ale. This was one of three types of tribute a Saxon 'boor' or peasant could be made to pay his lord for the land he farmed, the others being 'honey tribute' and 'meat tribute.'

The Anglo-Saxons recognized three types of ale, which are mentioned in old charters setting out land rents, that often had to be paid in food and drink. One type was *hlutres aloth*, clear ale; the second was *lithes aloth*, mild (or sweet) ale; and the third *Waelsces aloth*, Welsh ale. This last type was probably the same as bragget, or honey-beer. Clear ale was what later centuries would call stale or old ale, which had been left standing long enough to clear, by which time it would probably have acquired a slightly sour flavor (like a modern Belgian brown beer), while mild ale would still be fresh and unsoured.

## The ale-wife goes to Hell

The laws were harsh for brewers who failed to reach a decent standard. In Chester in the middle of the tenth century AD, any brewer who made bad beer was either put in the ducking-stool or fined four shillings, a considerable amount for the time. Most brewing at this time was done by women, as it was in Egyptian times and would be for another four hundred years. In the city of Hereford before the Normans came, 'any man's wife' who brewed ale 'inside or outside the city' paid ten pence as a customary due to the city authorities. Three hundred years later, in the reign of Edward III, a law was passed that banned men from having more than one trade, but 'women, that is to say, brewers, bakers, corders and spinners… may freely work as they have done before this time.' Ale-wives were regarded with much suspicion by the drinking public, however, who always feared they were being sold poor-quality produce, and short measure too. In one of the Chester mystery plays of the fourteenth century, the only soul not saved from purgatory is the ale-wife, who is carried off to Hell by demons.

The one place where men were found brewing was in the monasteries, which needed a large number of lay workers to maintain the monks, nuns, and priests. At the monastery of Bury St Edmunds in 1086, 35 priests, deacons, and clerics, and 28 nuns, and 'poor people' were looked after by 75 'bakers, brewers, tailors, washers, shoemakers, robemakers, cooks, porters, and bursars.' One of the biggest breweries in the medieval world was at the Abbey of St Gall in Switzerland (modern St Gallen), which had three separate brewhouses in the ninth century. It is believed each brewhouse made a different type of beer: one made only *prima melior* for distinguished guests and the fathers, another made *seconda* for lay brothers and the other monastery employees, and the third made *tertia* for pilgrims seeking lodgings and refreshment for the night.

The volume of ale consumed in the Middle Ages seems incredible today. Edward I, King of England from 1272 to 1307, had to supply his soldiers with around a gallon of ale a day. Much the same amount was drunk by ordinary householders, male and female. But water, especially in towns and cities, was unsafe to drink, and tea and coffee had not yet arrived. At least with ale the water had to be boiled first.

## The alestake and the Assize of Ale

Commercial brewers-for-sale, in England anyway, were supposed to put out a sign every time they brewed, the alestake, to let the official aletasters (or aleconners) know that they should come and sample the drink, to ensure it was good and up to strength. The price was regulated from at least the second half of the twelfth century by the Assize of Ale, a jury which sat to consider how much brewers should charge for their ale based on the local price of grain. There were fines for breaking the assize, which also stipulated what measures should be used, and what physical punishment could be inflicted upon offending brewers. Usually, as in Chester, this was the ducking stool. But the regularity with which many brewers were recorded as paying fines for breaking the assize suggests the 'fines' were used more as a license fee than a punishment.

There were certainly large numbers of commercial brewers. A trade list for St Albans of around 1360 mentions a total of 81 brewers, though

Left **The medieval Gruut Huis in Bruges, Belgium, where the herbal mixture used to flavor beer before hops arrived was sold.**

more than half (and probably all) also practiced on other trades. All seven of the inkeepers listed were also brewers. It is unlikely that any inn at this time would not have brewed its own ale. London in 1309 had 354 taverns and 1,334 brewers.

## The use of gruit in Germany and the Low Countries

Before the fourteenth century, ale was flavored with an assortment of herbs and spices, depending on what was available locally. One of the most popular plants used for flavoring ale was the moorland bush sweet gale, also known as bog myrtle. Sweet gale was one of the main ingredients in *gruit*, the mixture of herbs used to flavor ale in Germany and the Low Countries: other ingredients included yarrow and wild rosemary or marsh tea. The right to gather the herbs for *gruit* was often appropriated by the Church, which charged the manufacturers a sum known as *gruitgeld*. Brewers then had to buy this herbal mixture from the local *gruithaus*, which often – as in Bruges in Belgium – was a substantial and impressive building, due to the income derived from the monopoly on selling the only legal beer flavoring. The name *gruit* appears to be connected with words such as grits and groats, indicating the herbs were mixed with ground grain before being sold to the brewers. This was probably to disguise exactly what plants went into the mixture – certainly its composition was kept secret.

The first definite mention of hops in brewing comes in a work by the Abbess Hildegard of St Ruprechtsberg, near Bingen, in the Rhineland, who died in 1179. However, the Abbess mentions hops as only one of several herbs that could be used in flavoring beer. Over the next century brewers discovered that hops above all other plants, if boiled for two hours in the raw wort, not only gave a delicious flavor to the brew but also helped to preserve the beer from spoiling much longer than any other additive. By using hops, beer could be kept weeks, even months, without relying on alcoholic strength alone. The result was that, for the first time, beer could be traded outside the immediate area where it was brewed.

## Hopped beer becomes popular

In the thirteenth century hops began to be grown in substantial quantities in northern Germany, and the north German brewers in towns such as Hamburg and Bremen started to export their beer to places such as Holland, where hopped beer rapidly became very popular, despite opposition from the *gruit*-sellers. In 18 months between 1352 and 1354, 35,000 barrels of Hamburg beer were imported into Amsterdam. Hopped beer was made in many parts of Holland from around 1325. It was made in Bruges in 1351, and in Louvain by 1371. The Dutch began growing hops at the latest by 1360 or 1370 in Holland and North Brabant, and hop growing was taking place west of Brussels early in the next century. By 1415 the output of hopped beer in Louvain equalled that of *gruit* beer, and by 1435 hops had completely replaced *gruit* in the city.

Hopped beer began to be imported into England from the 1370s, and hops themselves were being imported by the 1420s: there were brewers of 'birra,' as distinct from 'cervisia' (ale) recorded at Hythe in Kent in 1419. But the trade was almost, if not completely in the hands of 'aliens,' foreigners mostly from The Netherlands and Flanders. This caused resentment among the native English, and in 1424/5 the London ale brewers made a complaint about 'aliens nigh to the city dwelling [who] brew beer and sell it to retail within the same city.'

art as hitherto, notwithstanding the malevolent attempts that were being made to prevent natives of Holland and Seland and others who occupied themselves in brewing the drink called biere from continuing their trade, on the ground that such drink was poisonous, and not fit to drink, and caused drunkenness, whereas it was a wholesome drink, especially in summer time.' Other cities, however, tried to ban the hop. For example hops were still being proscribed in Oxford, Coventry, and Leicester in the early 1520s, though all three places had beer brewers operating a few decades later. About 1525 the first hop gardens were planted in Kent, which has remained a center for English hop growing to this day.

Ale and beer continued to be separate drinks in England, brewed by different people, until at least the reign of James I in the early 1600s. In 1574 there were 58 large ale brewers in London, all English, and 32 large beer brewers, of whom 12 or so were foreigners and another six employed foreign-born workers. (The beer brewers, incidentally, may have been smaller in number but they had an average output more than three times that of the ale brewers.) Even in 1606 in the town of St Albans, three years after the death of Elizabeth I, the four beer brewers and two ale brewers who were licensed to brew by the corporation were kept separate.

## Royal writ to protect brewers

Eleven years later, in 1436, King Henry VI had to issue a Royal writ in London to try to stop the harassment of beer brewers in the city. The sheriffs were told to 'make proclamation for all brewers of biere within their bailiwick to continue to exercise their

## The origin of the word beer

The word beer had been found in Saxon English, but evidently meaning something different from ale. It came back into the language with the hopped drink. The ancestor of modern German once had a word like 'ale,' but this was replaced around the sixth or seventh centuries AD in West Germanic speech by *bior* (modern German *bier*), derived from the monastic Latin word *biber*, meaning drink generally. The new word spread into Dutch (*bier*), French (*bière*) and Italian (*birra*), and also to the Slavonic languages, where it became *pivo* (*piwo* in Polish), and as far away as China, where the word for beer is pronounced *pijiu*, and Japan, where it became *biiru*.

The opportunities for trade that the long-lived hopped beer presented meant that brewing was beginning to stop being mostly small-scale, and some substantial breweries were opening up. In London, Southwark, on the south side of the Thames, had become a center of brewing, while other 'great bere-houses' were operating at St Katharine's, just east of the Tower of London. In 1590, 20 large Thames-side breweries were exporting 26,400 barrels of beer a year. There had been 'common' brewers in the city, those who brewed 'commonly,' or regularly (*communiter* in Latin), and thus made a profession of it, from at least 1336. But these new beer brewers were on a different scale, and they formed part of the *nouveau riche* of Elizabethan England. The writer Robert Greene attacked them in 1592, declaring that they 'growe to be worth forty thousand pounds' by selling 'sodden water' (that is, boiled water), while they 'spare the malt and put in more of the hop.'

However, despite the rise of the rich Elizabethan brewer, remarkably few London breweries of later times could claim to have roots in Tudor businesses. The beer company Courage, whose brewery diagonally across the Thames from the Tower of London closed in 1981, claimed to be on the site of Vassal Webling's brewhouse, in existence in 1578. The Greenes, whose brewery in Pimlico, London, later became Watney's,

liked to say they were brewing at the Talbot Inn by the Great Gatehouse of the Abbey of Westminster in the early sixteenth century. The Reynolds family had been at the Hour Glass Brewery in Thames Street since at least the 1580s, but as the City of London Brewery Company the concern finally stopped brewing in 1936. The Red Lion brewery, in East Smithfield, London, which became famous under the Parsons – and, later, the Hoares, as a porter brewery – was on the site of a sixteenth-century brewhouse whose owners were said to be brewers to the court of Henry VIII. However it brewed its last beers in 1934. But those are all the breweries that can trace their history that far back, out of dozens of sixteenth-century London companies.

## Breweries that stood the test of time

The seventeenth century saw a few more breweries founded that were destined to last: the Anchor brewery at Southwark, later to become Barclay Perkins, was founded by James Monger around 1616 next door to the Globe theater. It closed when under the flag of Courage, in 1960. Joseph Truman was brewing in Black Eagle Street, Spitalfields, by the 1680s, in a brewery built about 1666, and only shut in 1989. Outside the City the Draper family was brewing in Wandsworth, Surrey, by 1675. The concern is still running as Young and Co. Further out, Hodgson's brewery in Kingston-upon-Thames, which claimed a foundation date of 1610, only closed in 1965.

The county of Kent was a good place for long-lived breweries. Thomas Tomson was brewing at Ramsgate in a brewery that had been founded in 1644/5, which finally closed 324 years later in 1968. The brewery that became Shepherd Neame in Faversham – still open today – was running in the 1680s. The brewery in Hythe, where Mackeson stout was first brewed (it is now brewed in London) claimed the foundation date of 1669. Moving to Norfolk, in Great Yarmouth the brewery that would become Lacon's was in operation by 1640, again closing only in 1968.

The north of England, however, and Scotland and Wales, were still lacking big brewers. The anonymous author of *A Guide to Gentlemen and Farmers for Brewing the Finest Malt Liquors*, published in 1703, explained that:

> *'in most, if not all of the Northern counties there are few or no common brewers. The Inn-Keepers and Publick Ale houses brewing what they retail in their own Houses. And Private Families for themselves. In the West of England they have some common brewers, but not in proportion to the East and South,'*

Left **An eighteenth-century brewhouse of the sort found in a large country home, showing copper and mash tun, fermenting vessel, and barrels, from the *Dictionarium Domesticum* of 1736.**

Left **The birth of porter is surrounded by more myth than any other event in brewing history.**

where almost all the inhabitants of the big towns and cities bought their drink from the common brewers. The author went on to describe the malt used by brewers in the West Country as:

> 'so stenched with the smoak of the wood with which 'tis dryed that no stranger can endure it, though its inhabitants, who are familiarized with it, can swallow it as the Hollanders do their thick black beer brewed with Buck Wheat.'

The author also described how:

> 'many country gentlemen talk of, and magnify their stale beer of 5, 10 or more years old ... I always broach mine at about nine months' end, that is, my March beer at Christmas and my October beer at midsummer, at which times it is generally at the best. But will keep very well in Bottles a year or two more.'

## The birth of porter

By this time London was supplied by 190 different common breweries, for a population of 600,000 people. But all were little better than craft brewers, their output limited by the existing technology. The average production was less than 10,000 barrels of beer a year. The big problem was the lack of a way to cool the brewhouse and the fermenting vessels. Too hot a fermentation meant spoilt beer, which meant output had to be limited. What came next was a lateral solution to the problem: a beer that could be brewed on a large scale using existing technology, but which still tasted good. That beer was porter.

The birth of porter is surrounded by more myth than any other event in brewing history. The traditional story says porter was first made around 1720 by a brewer named Ralph Harwood at his brewhouse in Shoreditch High Street, on the eastern edge of the City of London. The first public house to sell it, the story goes, was the Last in nearby Curtain Road (better known under the name and address it has had since its rebuilding in 1876, the Old Blue Last, Great Eastern Street).

Right **An inn in Knightsbridge, London, England, advertising Meux's 'entire,' or porter, and ale from the capital's biggest ale brewers, Goding's, of the Lion brewery, Lambeth, which closed in 1923.**

## Mild and stale, and twopenny, a strong pale ale

A rhyming guide to London's pubs written about 1715, the *Vade Mecum for Malt Worms*, contains the names of a host of different beers. Among the most frequently mentioned are mild and stale – that is, fresh beer and beer that has been allowed to mature – and twopenny, a strong pale ale. Others include amber, double beer, stout, 'humming stingo,' oat ale, October, Dorchester (at eight pence a quart, twice the price of twopenny), 'hocky,' Burton ale, Oxford ale, 'York's pale ale,' 'Bull's Milk Beer,' and 'full casks of Threads call'd Three.' Later writers say that Three Threads was a blend of three different types of beer – mild, stale, and twopenny – that had to be mixed in the pot by the landlord from three separate casks. The evidence from the *Vade Mecum for Malt Worms* suggests that Three Threads was actually ready-mixed in the cask by either the landlord or the brewer. Whatever the truth, the traditional story says Harwood called his new beer 'entire,' or 'entire butt' (a butt being a cask of about 126 gallons), to distinguish it from the blended beers popular at the time – one meaning of 'entire' is unmixed. (Another meaning of entire is stallion, the significance of which would probably not be lost on eighteenth-century drinkers.)

However, the new beer soon acquired the name porter, from its popularity with London's thousands of porters, the working-class population of the city who made their living from porterage – moving goods about the streets, on and off ships, and in and out of cellars and warehouses. Only brewers continued to call it entire.

# BLACK BEAUTY

GUINNESS

GUINNESS. PURE GENIUS

"I DON'T THINK I'LL LIKE IT."

GUINNESS EXTRA. ACQUIRE THE TASTE.

Left and middle **Two modern advertisements for Guinness stout, a descendent of the porter Arthur Guinness first brewed in the 18th century.** Above **Guinness is good for you and so is malt, even for nursing mothers, as this German label proclaims.**

There is no contemporary evidence to show that Ralph Harwood actually invented porter, only an account written nearly 70 years later which suggested he may have done so. There is evidence to suggest Harwood's brewery helped perfect the drink. However he was not a hugely successful brewer; at one point in the 1740s he and his business partner, James Harwood (presumably a brother or cousin), were declared bankrupt.

The drink, however, was a rapid success. Its first known mention comes in 1721, in a comment about dining at a cook's shop, 'upon beef, cabbage, and porter.' Five years later, the Frenchman César de Saussure, writing home from England to his family, said:

'In this country nothing but beer is drunk and it is made in several qualities. Small beer is what everyone drinks when thirsty; it is used even in the best houses and costs only a penny a pot. Another kind of beer is called porter... because the greater quantity of this beer is consumed by the working classes. It is a thick and strong beverage, and the effect it produces if drunk in excess, is the same as that of wine; this porter costs 3d the pot. In London there are a number of houses where nothing but this sort of beer is sold.'

## Knighthoods for brewers

The advantage of porter to brewers was that it was made from heavily scorched malt, which produced a robust dark beer that could be made in much larger quantities than the pale ales and ordinary brown beers that were previously all that was available. Indeed, porter positively demanded large-scale production: it took some months to mature properly, and to clear, and the brewers discovered that the larger the vessel porter was matured in, the better the drink. London's bigger brewers made huge fortunes from porter. There were knighthoods for

men such as Sir Benjamin Truman, Sir William Calvert, and Sir John Parsons, all leading porter brewers. By 1748 the 12 biggest porter brewers in London were selling more than 40 percent of all the capital's beer, with another 136 brewers fighting for the remainder. In 1796 London's biggest brewer, Whitbread, became the first brewery – probably – in the world to top 200,000 barrels a year, equal to more than one in ten of all pints brewed in the city.

Porter had, by this time, 'spread its fame half the world o'er.' The first porter brewery outside England's capital is believed to be the one advertised in the north in the *Leeds Mercury* newspaper in May 1744 by Thomas Elliott, who declared that at the Sheffield Brew House in Yorkshire he was now brewing porter 'warranted to be as good as any brew'd in London,' made by a trained brewer from a London porter brewery. The Old Porter Brewery in Bristol, in the southwest, was built in 1750. London porter brewers were in Dublin, Ireland, teaching their skills to the locals in 1763, and in Glasgow, Scotland, they were doing the same in 1775. The black beer was definitely being brewed in Dublin in 1780, when Patrick Sweetman was advertising Irish porter as 'equal if not superior to any English' at two guineas a hogshead, 'ready money only.' (A hogshead is equivalent to about 65 gallons.)

Robert Hare, whose father was a partner in Salmon and Hare's brewery in Stepney, east London (later Taylor Walker), emigrated to America and founded the first porter brewery in Philadelphia, possibly the first in North America, again in 1775. Hare's porter was a great favorite of George Washington, who would order 400 bottles at a time to be sent to his home at Mount Vernon. (Under various names, the brewery ran until 1939.) The first porter brewery in Sweden was founded in Göteborg in 1791 by William Knox. A year later William Beamish and William Crawford bought a brewery in Cork, Ireland, and renamed it the Cork Porter Brewery. It soon became the biggest brewery in Ireland, a position it kept until at least 1809, when it was brewing 100,000 barrels a year, 30,000 more than Guinness in Dublin.

Arthur Guinness had been brewing porter since around 1787. In 1799 he decided to stop brewing ale entirely, and concentrate on porter and its stronger version, brown stout. (Stout was originally an adjective meaning strong, so that stout beer meant strong beer of any color. Truman's brewery in east London had both brown and pale stout in stock in 1741. By the middle of the nineteenth century, however, stout meant a strong dark beer only.) Guinness prospered mightily in the third quarter of the nineteenth century, and became the biggest brewery in the world.

Early in the nineteenth century porter turned into a rather different product. As brewing science improved, brewers had discovered that the brown malt used for making porter was not very good value compared to the pale malt that went into lighter beers, because the browning process destroyed much of the fermentable sugars. The answer, from 1817 onward, was the use of black or patent malt, roasted like coffee, to give the beer color, and pale malt to give it body.

While the porter brewers were going over to patent malt, in the English Midlands a different style of beer was having problems. From the 1740s the brewers of Burton-upon-Trent had been exporting very strong, sweet beers to the Baltic via the River Trent and the port of Hull. Burton ale was 'the favorite drink of the better classes in every Baltic port from Hamburg to St Petersburg.' But the Napoleonic Wars had badly damaged the trade, and when it picked up again after the French Emperor's defeat at Waterloo, the Russians then imposed impossible import tariffs on foreign beer.

## The story of India Pale Ale

In 1822 one of the leading Burton brewers, Samuel Allsopp was dining in London with Campbell Marjoribanks, a director of the East India Company, which controlled trade between Britain and India. Allsopp was complaining about the collapse of the Russian market. 'Why not make an attempt on the India market?' Marjoribanks asked. 'I never heard of it,' Allsopp replied. The East India Company man explained that 5,000 hogsheads of English beer were sent to Madras and Bengal every year, almost all of it brewed by a London brewer called Hodgson. The Indian climate was too hot for

Left **A trade advertisement from the early twentieth century, when small brewers were just beginning to start supplying their beers in bottles.**

brewing using the technology of the time, and there was no risk of tariffs being imposed on imports. Hodgson's India Ale was almost the generic name in the trade. But Hodgson, whose brewery stood by the River Lea at Bow, just east of London, had 'given offence to most of our merchants in India,' who would welcome a new supplier.

Marjoribanks told Allsopp that his current Burton ale, 'so strong and sweet,' would not suit the Indian market, but if he could reproduce Hodgson's beer 'it will be a fortune to you.' A few days later, back at his brewery in Burton, Samuel Allsopp received from Marjoribanks a hamper containing a dozen bottles of Hodgson's ale, together with a joking note about 'coals to Newcastle.' Allsopp got his maltster, Job Goodhead, to make malt of the right color, and the first consignment of 12 butts and 14 hogsheads of Allsopp's pale ale for India, just over 2,400 gallons, went out east on December 27, 1823. (A butt is equivalent to about 126 gallons and a hogshead is roughly 65 gallons.)

India ale was a highly hopped strong beer designed to survive the long journey round Africa. Along the way it had to cope with high temperatures and much shaking about in the holds of the sail-powered East Indiamen as they twice crossed the Equator – there was, of course, no Suez Canal to shorten the journey. Although the Hodgsons had an effective monopoly by dint of being the first into the market, the semihard Thames basin water their brewery used was much less suited to producing a bright, pale, bitter beer than the heavily sulphate-laden well waters of the Trent valley, where Burton was. Burton pale ale was soon recognized in India as a superior brew to Hodgson's. Allsopp and the other Burton brewers, including Bass and Worthington, quickly took the market off the Londoners.

Left **Taylor Walker, founded in 1730, was originally Salmon and Hare's brewery in Stepney, east London, England.**

## India Pale Ale finds a new market

The new ale was, at first, as much an export-only beer as the old Baltic brew had been. It is supposed to have become popular in Britain only after a ship loaded with around 300 hogsheads (that's 19,500 gallons) of India Pale Ale that had just set out from Liverpool was wrecked in the Irish Sea in 1827. The salvaged cargo, or what there was left of it, was sold locally to pay the underwriters, and those who got to try it immediately asked for more. India Pale Ale was particularly popular with the middle-class beer drinker, who was delighted with its sparkling clarity and crisp bitter taste, and IPA became the fashionable drink of the nineteenth century in Great Britain.

In Germany, meanwhile, the emphasis was still on dark beers, though this was about to change dramatically. Like porter, many German beers were stored for some time to mature. The German for store is *lager*, and these beers were thus known as *lager-bier*. In the mountainous south, where there were cold caves in which to store beer, it was thought that a different strain of yeast sprang into prominence in these cold conditions. This yeast worked away at the bottom of the fermenting vessel, unlike other yeasts which preferred a warmer environment. For this reason they were called bottom-fermenting yeasts, and it is the differently acting yeasts that distinguishes today's lagers from beers such as IPA, stout, bitter and other styles made with top-fermenting yeasts.

The brewers of Bavaria found that beers brewed with bottom-fermenting yeast were more stable, and kept better than top-fermented beers. They were evangelists for the style, and other brewers in Germany, the Austrian Empire, and Scandinavia began to brew using bottom-fermenting yeasts too. The first brewery in Sweden making a Munich-style beer opened in 1843. The year before, a group of pub brewers in Plzen, Bohemia (Pilsen in German), had decided to start their own large-scale brewery, and invited a Bavarian brewer, Josef Groll, to come and run it for them, bringing with him some of that bottom-fermenting yeast.

## The very first Pilsner lager

What Groll produced for the Bohemians must have been a surprise to everybody, perhaps even a surprise to himself. The new brewery's maltings were based on British ideas, producing a pale, IPA-style malt.

Above **One of four lithographs issued by the Stroh Brewery Co., Detroit, sometime between 1900 and 1903. Bernard Stroh opened in Detroit in 1850.**

Plzen's soft water, in any case, meant little color came out of the malt into the beer. The local barley was low in protein and plenty of hops were used, which would have helped make the beer clear and sparkling. Groll presented the brewery's owners, not with the dark Munich-style lager they were probably expecting, but with a pale golden beer, the very first Pilsner lager.

The production of pale lager spread to other towns in Bohemia, notably Ceské Budejovice (Budweis in German). Budweis was one of the places visited by the American brewer Adolphus Busch on trips to Europe in the late 1860s and early 1870s. Back home in St Louis in 1876 he launched a brew he called Budweiser Lager Beer. Twenty years later this was followed by a beer named for another central European town – Michelob in Slovakia.

In America the first settlers – British and Dutch – had kept their homegrown preferences for top-fermented beers. The first known brewery in what was to become the United States opened in the Dutch colony of New Amsterdam (now Manhattan) in 1612. Eight years later, a brewhouse was among the first structures built by the English settlers at Plymouth in the Colony of Massachusetts in the winter of 1620/21.

By 1810 the now-independent young country had 132 commercial breweries, the majority in New York and Philadelphia, for a population of around seven million. In 1829 David G. Yuengling opened a brewery in Pottsville, Pennsylvania, which survives today as the oldest brewery in the United States. (It is not, however, the oldest brewery company in North America; that title goes to Molson, founded in Montreal in 1786 by John Molson from Lincolnshire, England.)

# America's first lager

All America's brewers were ale brewers, however, until 1840, when a small brewer in Philadelphia, John Wagner, brewed the continent's first known lager. The likelihood is that, before then, German immigrants to America had been unable to bring bottom-fermenting yeast across the Atlantic because it died on the long journey. Faster sailing ships, particularly the clippers in use from the early 1830s, cut the journey time and enabled the yeast to get from Europe to America while it was still viable.

Wagner was too small to make a success of the new beer, but within a few years other brewers had started making lager in America: Jacob Best began a brewery in Milwaukee in 1844, encouraged by the ice for lagering which could be got from Lake Michigan. The firm eventually took the name of Jacob's granddaughter's husband, Frederick Pabst, and the Pabst brewery in Milwaukee closed only in 1997. August Krug began brewing in Milwaukee in 1849. His concern was to become the Schlitz operation. A year later the country could boast 431 breweries, one being the newly opened company of Bernard Stroh in Detroit. Within a decade this had risen to 1,269 breweries, and by 1873 the total had reached a peak of 4,131. From then, however, the numbers would start to fall.

Many of the operations that would close over the coming decades were America's ale brewers, as lager took a grip of the nation's palate. It took 40 years for lager sales in America to pass those of ale, but advances in refrigeration and yeast control slowly brought a better lager to the consumer, one with which the ale brewers found they could

not compete. The last ale brewer in Milwaukee closed in 1880. By 1910 the number of brewers in the United States had dropped to 1,500.

# The prohibition years

The passing of a bill in 1919 to outlaw alcoholic drink was, of course, a hammer-blow to brewers in the United States. Some kept going by brewing 'near beer,' making non-alcoholic drinks such as malted milk and soda, even making cheese. A year after the repeal of Prohibition in 1933, only 756 breweries had reopened. By 1940 beer production was at preProhibition levels, but with only half the number of breweries. Mergers and takeovers were thinning out the breweries that had survived. Between 1949 and 1958, 185 American breweries closed or sold out. By 1961 there were only 230 breweries in operation, of which just 140 were independently-owned. In 1977 the number had fallen to fewer than 100.

However, that same year America's first 'microbrewery,' the New Albion Brewery in Sonoma, California, brewed its first beers. This brewery only lasted until the early 1980s, but the movement it started has grown like a balloon. There were 400 new breweries by 1994 and more than 1,000 today, so now the United States can finally boast more breweries than Bavaria.

While Plzen was developing pale lager, brewers in Britain were refining a style inspired by IPA, but less strong. This was given the name bitter beer or bitter ale, and one of the earliest references to it comes in an advertisement by Edward and John Samuel Nanson of the Lady's Bridge Brewery, Sheffield, south Yorkshire in 1852 for 'Ale, Porter, and Bitter Beer.' By 1875, at the latest, the drink was referred to solely as bitter. At the same time another style was being perfected by British brewers. It was darker, sweeter, and less hopped than bitter, and was sold under the name mild ale, or mild. In its earliest incarnation, mild was not necessarily a weak beer, but by the beginning of the twentieth century it was normally weaker as well as sweeter than bitter.

While the rest of the world fell to the advance of pale, Pilsner-style lagers, British beer drinkers stuck to mild and bitter. Australia's first lager producer, the Gambrinus brewery, was opened by a couple of German entrepreneurs in Melbourne in 1885. However, Australia's first really successful lager brewery was established by the Foster brothers from New York, who started their brewery in Collingwood, Victoria, in 1888. Today even those beers regarded in Australia as bitters, such as Castlemaine XXXX, are brewed lager-style, with bottom-fermenting yeast.

In Britain, meanwhile, the first lager brewers had little success. The Austro-Bavarian Beer Company, the very first specialist lager brewer in the country, began brewing in Tottenham, north London in 1882, but closed finally in 1903. The Wrexham Lager Brewery Company started in

1883, and continued largely by going for the export market. In Scotland, Tennent's brewery in Glasgow opened a lager plant in 1885, but it was to be 90 years before lager sales in Scotland overtook those of ales.

One type of beer that did do well in Britain was a carbonated, pressurized version of draft beer (spelt draught in the UK) known as keg. The United States Army Air Force played a part in its development: from 1943 onwards there were many American airmen stationed in the south Midlands, particularly in the county of Bedfordshire, because American bombers were beginning to strike at Hitler's Germany from bases in Britain. However, the thirsty USAAF personnel did not take to the traditional English draft ale, and that was mostly all they could buy locally. It was much too warm and flat for their lager-conditioned palates. What they did like were the sharper bottled beers. But because of the war bottles, like so much else, were rationed.

## JW Green rescues thirsty Americans

The commanders of the US forces, led by General Curtis Le May, turned to their nearest big brewer, JW Green of Luton, Bedfordshire, and promised to supply the company with all the necessary malt and hops if they could provide an answer to their problem. The solution was not entirely new, however, because Watney, the London brewer, had been experimenting with something similar in the 1930s. But what JW Green did with the Americans' ingredients was to brew a beer that was then chilled, filtered, and put into special casks under pressure; it was 'bottled beer from barrels.' Trucks from far-off USAAF bases made long journeys to Luton to pick up supplies. No delay was allowed before the beer got to the lips of the gallant US airmen returning from action, the local newspaper reported.

*'The special serving apparatus which is needed for the beer, including an icebox for the cask, is fitted onto jeeps, and when the great bombers touch down after smashing at the Hun, out dash the jeeps with a drink for the crews.'*

A few years after the war was over, the idea was revived, and the new beer – dubbed 'keg' beer – began to oust traditional handpumped beer from the bartops of Britain's pubs.

Even in the 1950s, lager was still regarded as an alien drink in Britain. One writer in 1949 declared: 'Lager is not a very popular drink in pubs, except in fairly high-class saloon bars during very hot weather. One can usually get bottled lager but it is not always iced.' It was not until the 1960s, with the launch of Harp lager (by a consortium led by Guinness) and Skol (originally brewed in Scotland), and the success of the Canadian lager Carling Black Label in Britain, that the beer that had captured the rest of the world finally started to have an impact in Britain. By 1990 lager in all its forms – draft, bottled, and canned – had finally captured the majority of the UK beer market, with sales of 51.4 percent.

Top **The ultimate collectible – a 1924 Daimler 'bottle van,' putting a White Shield pale ale 'bottle' to original use. National Motor Museum, Beaulieu, England.**
Above **A magnificent display of more traditional brewery transport, the horse-drawn dray, with beautifully groomed "Kaltblüter" horses, from a collectible postcard issued by Germany's Feldschlossen brewery.**

Britain, like the United States, had seen the number of operating breweries tumble since the nineteenth century. The country had around 2,000 brewing companies at the start of World War I. By 1940 this had crashed to 428. The number had fallen further, to 247 brewing companies in 1960, and hit a low in 1972 with 95 brewing companies operating around 145 breweries, and just four surviving pub breweries. That year the first new small brewery in Britain opened, in Selby, north Yorkshire, England. A new interest in beer was stimulated by the rise of the Campaign for Real Ale, or Camra. It was founded in 1971 as a reaction against the rise of 'keg' beer, which was considered tasteless and unpleasant compared to traditional cask ales by Camra members. Camra quickly attracted tens of thousands of members who were keen to try more interesting beers. Since then Britain's microbrewery revolution has seen hundreds of new brewers open their doors, and today more than 350 are still in operation.

# Collecting beer memorabilia is fun

'BEER, THE BEST LONG DRINK IN THE WORLD.' Millions would agree with that slogan, adopted in Britain as part of a campaign to promote beer. This was launched in the same week in December 1933 that Prohibition ended in the United States. Today, from Peking to Patagonia, Norway to New Zealand, in the bars of San Francisco, and the taverns of old Prague, you'll find people enjoying beer, the globe's most popular alcoholic drink.

Where there is beer, there are bottles and cans, glasses, mugs and steins, coasters and beer mats, beer fonts, pump clips, ashtrays, mirrors and posters, labels, bottle tops, even T-shirts and ties – all bearing the name of a brewery or beer. All, as large numbers of enthusiasts will testify, are eminently collectable. Few drinkers haven't slipped a coaster or beermat into their pocket as a memento of a great night out, or stuck an empty bottle or beer can up on a shelf. It might be kept as a reminder of a favorite ale, a home-town brew or an exotic holiday far away, or in admiration of its rarity or design. You might like the history of beer; the history of beer styles; or perhaps you just like beer.

Collecting beer memorabilia can teach you history (how India Pale Ale came about, for example), geography (there are breweries in almost every country around the world; even Baghdad has a brewery), and foreign languages (learn the Danish for Easter beer and the Welsh for 'red dragon,' trademark of several of the principality's brewers). It can also, like all good hobbies, make you plenty of new friends. There are clubs and societies in many countries for collectors of cans, bottles, labels, coasters and so on, while the Internet will put you in touch with collectors from all over the world.

Enthusiasts have identified more than 50 different areas of beer memorabilia collecting. You don't have to collect the obvious cans, bottles, or coasters. There are brewery tokens, like the ones Theakston hands out to people who visit its brewery in north Yorkshire to entitle them to a free pint in the brewery bar, or the ones given away by breweries at Mardi Gras time in New Orleans. There are waiter trays, from the beautiful examples of early-twentieth-century America, with ladies in diaphanous dresses advertising their favorite beer, to the plainer types of today. Badged glasses

are popular with many collectors, especially now the flood of new microbreweries from the United States to New Zealand is providing new names to collect. Some people like to collect the cardboard packs in which canned or bottled beers are sold. They are usually highly colorful, since they are designed to catch the eye in a busy supermarket.

Font or tap handles and, in the UK especially, pump clips, have specialists who can show you collections of 1,000 or more. Again, the microbrewery boom means a continuing flood of new types. Brewery giveaways that have proved collectable include pencils (more than 170 different brewery pencils are known in the United States), playing cards (there is a brewery collectors' society for decks of cards), bags (both paper and plastic), golf balls and golf tees, and matchboxes and matchbooks (or matchcovers, as the specialists prefer to call them).

You can even dress yourself head to toe in breweriana. Some enthusiasts have made jackets and waistcoats out of bar towels, but brewers themselves have put their names on T-shirts, sweatshirts, baseball jackets, caps, and even (as with the Firkin pub brewery chain in the UK) socks and underpants. Brewery neckties, in particular, attract collectors, with the biggest collections topping the 500 mark. To go with the ties there are cufflinks and tiepins, and lapel badges are a complete new field again.

# How to collect

THIS BOOK COVERS beer-related collectables of every kind, with an emphasis on the contemporary, the easily affordable, and the easily obtainable. Some people will pay thousands for some rare and old item, but you can derive equal pleasure from collecting items that cost very little or are free even. Where do you start? At your local bar or pub, of course, over a glass of beer.

The owner or manager of your local might know you already, which is a good start. There are a couple of rules to remember, however. If you wish to take anything – even just a coaster or beermat – ask the bar staff first. Removing any item from the premises without first gaining permission to do so is theft. So, remember to ask and offer to pay for anything more valuable than a coaster, such as an ashtray.

Once the beer memorabilia bug has taken hold of you, then you'll want to meet other collectors by joining a club, and this will soon become perhaps the best source of material. Clubs are often the only way. All clubs hold regular meetings, either locally or nationally. Here you will be able to swap or buy, exchange gossip, even have a beer. Most, if not all, clubs also have regular newsletters or magazines, with advertisements from members offering items to sell or swap, so if you cannot get to a meeting you need not feel left out. Clubs also enable you to get in touch with collectors overseas, so that you can swap items from your country for items from theirs: collectors in Eastern Europe are particularly keen to set up swapping arrangements.

Many collectors' clubs have deals with breweries so that mats and coasters or bottle labels can be distributed in bulk through the club. Otherwise, you can try writing direct to breweries: but many, especially the new microbreweries, are too busy running their businesses to deal with mail from collectors, and who can blame them? Again, clubs often have address lists of breweries to write to who will respond to requests for coasters or labels.

The Internet is another good place to make contacts: many collectors' clubs have websites, some of them as good as or better than anything produced by the big brewers themselves. Many collectors also have their own websites, where they have placed scans of items from their collections, and some breweriana and beer memorabilia dealers also advertise on the Net.

Collectors' fairs, which generally cover an enormous range of items from china dolls to old postcards, are a good place to find beer memorabilia, especially framed signs, mirrors, jugs, waiter trays, and the like. But while you can find bargains, the really desirable stuff is usually very expensive. Breweriana sometimes comes up at auction: Sotheby's in London, the big auction house, has had a couple of sales of

Guinness collectibles in recent years. Again, however, the prices are often well outside the pocket of most collectors. There are also specialist ephemera fairs, where you can find old billheads, flyers, even posters, photographs, and deeds to brewery property.

If you're looking for cheaper ways to find rarer items, secondhand stores, junk shops, thrift shops and charity shops are all good sources for beer memorabilia. Sometimes you can pick up items such as ashtrays that are 40 or 50 years old and advertise a long-gone brewery for just a few pennies. There are also specialist breweriana stores, especially in the United States, where you can find practically anything you might be looking for.

You can also advertise in your local newspaper for people who have brewery memorabilia they would like to sell to contact you. This is a great way to collect older items if you have a brewery that existed until recently in your town, since former brewery workers are always a good source of collectibles. It can be tricky agreeing on a price, since often neither you nor the person selling the item has any idea what similar examples go for. The only answer to the price problem is that something is worth what you are prepared to pay for it and the seller is prepared to accept for it. If the two match up, you're in business. Sometimes, however, you can be offered something that is highly desirable but impossible to take. Once I was offered over the phone a complete etched pub window, which I had to turn down, since displaying it properly would have meant knocking part of the front of my house down! Even I had to draw the line there.

Below **The beginnings of a fine collection. Let the beer memorabilia bug get a hold on you.**

# Advertising materials

The first beer advertising was the ale stake, the pole put outside a building to announce ale had just been brewed inside. It seems to date from Saxon times. There is what looks like an ale stake depicted near a burning house on the Bayeux Tapestry, which recorded the victory of the Normans over the English in 1066.

The ale stake was designed as an indicator to the ale conner or ale taster that he should come and test the brew. The ale conner was a town or manorial official whose job was to ensure that all ale sold locally was of a good quality, and the measures used to dispense it were accurate. The stake became a sign for everybody that ale was on sale: Chaucer, who died in 1400, has his Pardoner say just before his contribution to *The Canterbury Tales*:

'"But first," quod he, "heere at this ale stake
I wol bothe drynke and eten of a cake."'

The stake was frequently decorated with a garland, known as the ale-bush, which was still in use at the end of the sixteenth century. Indeed, one writer on inn signs, Jacob Larwood, claimed in 1866 that in the western United States, when a new settlement was erected it was common to see a bunch of hay or a green bough hung from above the bar-room door, 'until such time as a superior decoration could be provided.' At least one brewer, Harman's of Uxbridge, on the edge of London, later used the ale garland as its trademark.

As brewing became less of an occasional trade marked by the need for one-off indications that ale was on sale, and more the province of 'common' brewers (that is, those who brewed 'commonly,' or all the time), the need for the ale stake disappeared. Also, there is little indication that common brewers publicized their beers before the eighteenth century. However as porter became the popular brew in England, the various big porter brewers began securing exclusive deals with taverns and public houses to supply their wares (the first 'tied houses'), and erected signboards on the front of the inns declaring that their beers were on sale inside. An engraving from the beginning of the nineteenth century of the White Hart in Knightsbridge, London, shows it with two signs, one for 'H. Meux and Co's Entire' and the other for 'Goding's fine XXX ale,' with Goding's cannon trademark.

Making up the signboards that advertised whose beer was on sale inside was the job of an entire department at London's biggest breweries. A description of a visit to Barclay Perkins in Southwark, on the south side of the Thames, in 1841 described, 'a building where Barclay, Perkins and Co.'s Entire stared us in the face in all shapes, colours and sizes; some boards higher than they were wide, others wider than high; some flat, some convex; some with gold letters on a green board, others on red. These were the inscription-boards, so well known in the London streets … which inform us whose "Entire" is sold by the publican. One shop is devoted to the carpenters who prepare the boards, and another to the painters and gilders who finish them.'

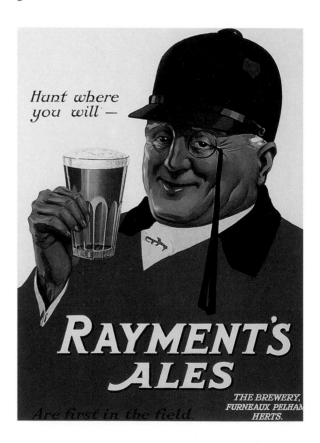

Above **The huntsman gets everywhere. This poster, from the printers Joseph Causton and Sons, was designed in 1921 and sold to three different English brewers, in the north (Tetley of Leeds), the southwest (Eldridge Pope), and the southeast (Rayment's of Furneux Pelham, a little village in east Hertfordshire). Eldridge Pope had its version redrawn in 1935, but Rayment's used the design until at least 1951. Today it is the exclusive trade mark of Tetley. Note the spelling mistake – Causton's put an extraneous 'a' in Furneux.**

Above **A superb art nouveau poster by Josette Boulanger for Brasseries de la Meuse, a brewery in eastern France which disappeared in the mid-1960s.**

Occasionally brewers would put out flyers or posters to advertise their beer. One rare survivor from Dublin in 1780 is for Pat Sweetman's Irish porter, brewed at the Porter Brewery, Stephen's Green, and for sale at two guineas per hogshead, 'for ready money only.' At the same time advertisements were appearing in local newspapers from brewers promoting their beers. In November 1792, for example, Conrad Hoburg of Gorsuch's Brewery in Baltimore, Maryland, paid for a notice to say that 'the subscriber respectfully informs his friends, and the public in general, that he has commenced brewing for the season … good wholesome Beer, by the barrel, gallon, or smaller quantity, at one shilling per gallon.'

Advertisements continued to be written in this almost apologetic manner for 70 or 80 years more. Two adjacent advertisements in October 1864 from the *Hertfordshire Express*,

the local newspaper in the little Home Counties market town of Hitchin, some 35 miles north of London, give the flavor. In one advertisement, the town's biggest brewer, J, W, and S Lucas,

> 'beg respectfully to invite the attention of their Friends and the Public to their Stock of Pale and Mild Ales, Porter and Stout, which are now in fine condition. Their genuine quality, agreeable flavour and moderate price, are especially worthy of notice.'

Immediately below, the Lucases' smaller rival, William Lewin, who had just moved to the Triangle brewery, Hitchin,

> 'returns his sincere thanks for the support he has received since his commencement in Business as a Brewer, and respectfully informs the gentry and public generally that he has removed to the above premises, (late the occupation of Mr William Richardson, Coachbuilder,) where by increased accommodation he will be enabled to supply Home-Brew'd Ales of the finest quality.'

Generally newspaper advertisements were simple listings of the beers made by the brewery, and their prices. Sometimes particular claims of purity were hinted at. For example an advertisement from the *Daily Eastern Argus* in Portland, Maine, in 1871 from J and P McGlinchy of the Casco brewery in Fore Street, declared:

> 'Having procured the services of an experienced Brewer we are now prepared to offer to the market an Ale, which we warrant pure. The Stock used being the very

Right **An attempt by the Chattanooga Brewing Co of Tennessee, which ran from 1890 to 1915, to express visually the wide range of beers available from the company.**

# Advertising materials

best quality, and the water Pure Sebago. We would respectfully call the attention of invalids where Ale is recommended by physicians.'

By now brewers were also using showcards and other point-of-sale advertising material. A drawing by the artist Hablot Knight Browne – known as 'Phiz,' for Charles Dickens's *Pickwick Papers*, published in 1837, includes a showcard for 'Guines's Dublin Stout' (sic) in the background of the public house scene where Sam Weller is reading out to his father, Tony, his newly composed valentine. The Guinness showcard appears plain and unillustrated, but the early existence of colored brewers' point-of-sale material is shown by a card from 1831 for Walker's of Warrington, a brewer from the north-west of England, showing drinkers in the brewery sample room, which was reproduced on a poster of 1883 now in the Public Record Office at Kew, London.

At the Centennial Exhibition in Philadelphia in 1876, brewers presented showcards made of glass and iron. Eventually these became the enamel signs, suitable for erecting outside pubs and

bars and at places such as railway stations. These are avidly collected today under the name 'street jewelry.'

## NATIONAL CHARACTERISTICS AND ONE COMMON THEME

Improvements in color printing, meanwhile, were bringing what might be called the 'golden age' of brewery advertising. From the 1880s, commercial artists in America and Europe produced gorgeous illustrations to publicize the wares of hundreds of brewers, small and large. Each country developed its own individual style. In America, jolly Germanic cartoon illustrations were popular, as were female beauties in drapery. The British went for flat, bright colors and illustrations which, even then, recalled a more settled social order: the parson, the master of the hunt, and the squire riding up to the village inn for a glass of ale, for example, or John Bull studying his bottle of beer with pleasure. In France in the late 1890s and early 1900s some of the best-known art nouveau artists, such as Alphonse Maria Mucha, were producing stunningly beautiful posters advertising the beers of the

Right **Plenty is going on in this poster from the Huizhou brewery in China.**

Meuse area. One theme common to all countries was the brewery illustration; the full-color print showing where the beer was made.

After World War I, beer advertising in America, of course, disappeared until the repeal of Prohibition. Elsewhere the poster rarely recovered the artistic vivacity of the pre-World War I years, the great exception being Guinness, whose posters in the 1930s quickly became classics. Some brewers took pride in ignoring publicity. For example Colonel Briggs, chairman of the British brewery Benskin's of Watford until his death aged 80 in August 1951, always refused to advertise. His obituary said that he had declined to advertise Benskin's 'except in a very small way,' and he had cut all advertising from the sides of Benskin's pubs and drays except for the company's name.

Newspaper and magazine advertising entered a dull period, epitomized by the full-page advertisements from the British brewer Whitbread in the *Illustrated London News* during the 1930s showing famous actors of the time,

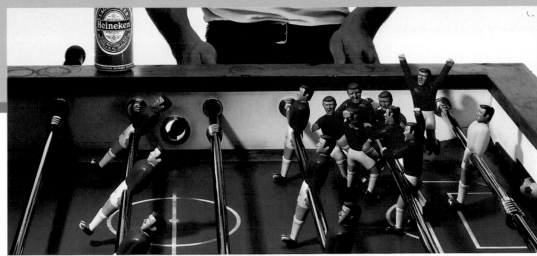

**Only Heineken can do this.**

Right **One of a series of posters from a highly-regarded campaign in the 1980s for Heineken in Britain shows the magical effect the beer has on a table-football game of the kind once found in many British pubs.**

such as Gertrude Lawrence and Ronald Squire, in full evening wear pretending to enjoy a glass of pale ale over supper at a high-class restaurant, an unlikely scene designed to try to raise the social profile of beer drinking.

Some beer advertising still captured the public heart, however. Liebmann Breweries, of Brooklyn, ran their 'Miss Rheingold campaign' for more than 25 years. It attracted a regular 15 million to 20 million votes each year, more than any other election except for the United States Presidency. Much beer advertising from the 1930s through 1970s is terrific material for the social historian: the smiling husband turning from the refrigerator full of Schlitz and declaring, 'Bless her heart!' for example.

## INTRODUCTION OF NEW MEDIA

Perhaps posters suffered because advertisers now had new media. The neon sign was replacing the painted sign outside many bars. In America, brewers were soon using radio to push their beers, with advertising spots, and sponsored shows such as Groucho Marx's *Blue Ribbon Town* for Pabst, which started in 1943. When television arrived, beer advertising followed onto the small screen, though there were worries about the impact of plugs for alcohol reaching right into people's living-rooms. In 1952 a House of Representatives sub-committee, responding to protests, investigated 'offensive' and 'immoral' TV programs, and looked at beer spots, as well as more possibly contentious items.

American brewers have always been good at translating radio and TV commercials into collectibles. The characters Bert and Harry Piel, for example, first appeared in radio and TV spots from 1955 in the New York area, advertising Piel's Real Draft. They were played by the comedians Bob Elliott and Ray Goulding, and TV listings slots would actually print the times their commercials were on air, so that fans – their fan club topped 100,000 members – would not miss them. By 1963 the pair had been turned into a

foot-high plastic bank or money box. Similarly with the Budweiser frogs, which hopped onto American TV screens in the 1990s, thanks to the skills of Stan Winston. In 1995 the three frogs were released as a three-inch-high ceramic pond scene, with a tiny 'Budweiser' sign in the background.

Humor has been the weapon used by many British brewers from the 1970s onward, though there are very few collectors preserving examples for the future. Almost all the best advertising has been for lager brands, and it is a fact that almost all British beer memorabilia collectors are real ale fans with a strong dislike for drinks they see as ersatz and alien to the country's beery traditions. As a result, although slogans such as 'refreshes the parts other beers cannot reach' from Heineken are very well known in Britain, advertisements depicting these slogans are going to be very rare in collections in future decades.

Some collectors have tapes of TV and radio commercials, which never fail to entrance people who remember, say, the Hamm's bear from St Paul, Minnesota, and its tag-line, 'From the land of sky blue waters' when it first appeared in 1954, or the animated Guinness zoo animals from the earliest days of television advertising in Britain. (There is obviously something about beer advertising and animals: at least three brewers – Guinness, Anheuser Busch, and Britain's John Smith's – have used penguins to plug their beers.) One recent new form of beer advertising is the computer screen saver, of which there are now several examples. The big problem here is that you have to save the computer that the screen saver was designed to run on, as well!

However, most advertising collectibles come in more solid form, as showcards, posters, mirrors, and 'back bar' items. They are found at collectors' fairs, in specialist shops, and occasionally at antique markets, while you might be lucky and pick up something at a garage sale. Do not turn something down just because it is recent: today's common piece is tomorrow's collectible.

# Posters - featuring women

**Above** Slightly battered but still gorgeous, this framed poster for the Brasserie de Champigneulles is typical of French beer advertising before World War I.

**Top right** The lovely 'Bohemian Girl' was designed in 1890 by Louis Prang, a famous lithographer from Boston, Massachusetts. She appears on at least two different posters issued by Stroh's of Detroit, advertising Bohemian Beer, as here, and Stroh's Extra, as well as on a poster for Born & Co. of Columbus, Ohio, where she advertised XX Pale Beer.

**Right** A splendidly Germanic young woman advertises Munich's Hacker-Pschorr brewery.

**Above** A lively pre-World War I poster from the Poretti brewery in Varese, Italy, where the young woman seems to have had too much of the product.

**Below** Reflecting the taste in the 1890s for an hour-glass body shape, this young woman is advertising one of the breweries that came together to form the Maryland Brewing Co. in 1899.

**Above** Nudity was acceptible before World War I if it could be made semi-mythical as with this little winged fairy advertising a non-alcoholic malt extract from Schlitz of Milwaukee.

**Above** 1980s beer advertising, as in this poster from Stroh, gave a rather different picture of young women than the one found 90 years earlier in brewery ads.

**Below** Robustly masculine 1930s advertising from the Australian brewer Tooth's of Sydney, later taken over by the company known best for Foster's.

**Above** The gathering of men depicted on this 1904 calendar from the David Stevenson Brewing Co. of New York, was clearly meant to indicate that the brewery's beers appealed to all classes. When Prohibition came in, the company used part of its refrigerated plant for storing furs.

**Above** There can never have been a simpler advertising slogan than this, from the series of porters in the 'Beer is Best' campaign put out by the British Brewers' Society from the 1930s through 1950s. See the pleasure on the man's face, and the glass he is using is the classic ten-sided pint.

**Right** The chaps in this 1930 poster for Newcastle Brown Ale are drinking from classic footed half-pint English bottled ale glasses.

**Below** Two gray-haired old fellows of the kind few modern brewers would use in their advertising promote the Channel Islands' brewer Randall's of Guernsey in the 1960s.

**Above** Enjoy it at home and in the bar is the clear message in this 1950s German poster from the Feldschlösschen brewery in Brunswick.

**Below** The brewery worker in this mid-twentieth century advert from Carling of Denmark looks worried enough to be the real thing.

# Posters – featuring adults & children

**Below** No one today would dare use images of small children to sell beer, but around 1901 this little girl was one of a series of lithographed advertisements from Stroh's brewery of Detroit featuring toddlers. Note the two beers featured in the ad: brown stout, very much in the British brewing tradition, and 'Bohemian beer,' a central European-style pale lager.

**Above** An Austrian gentleman dreams of a giant glass of lager surrounded by happy 1920s party folk in a poster from the Gosser brewery in Leoben-Goss.

**Above** The tide of fashion has meant the 'modern' couple in this 1970s advertisement for Vieux Temps pale ale from Belgium look more out of date than the smart pair from the 1930s beside them.

**Above** 'Don't drink the water, you don't know what's in it' is the warning on this poster from the Cerveceria Nacional in Bolivia.

# Posters - featuring animals

**Above** An example of this magnificent sign from DG Yuengling & Son's brewery – founded in Pottsville, Pennsylvania, in 1829 and thus the oldest operating brewery in the United States – sold for $4,500 a few years ago when it came up in a beer memorabilia auction.

**Below** The Buckeye Brewing Co. of Toledo, Ohio, cheered up the pre-Prohibition bars where its beer was served with this lovely poster, which came in a superb decorated frame. Buckeye survived until the 1950s.

**Above** One of several breweries owned by the great Austrian brewer Anton Dreher was the Köbánya brewery in Budapest, Hungary, for whom this fine poster was drawn by the Hungarian artist Endre Sárossy in 1923. Sör is the Hungarian for beer, and bak means bock, or goat, bock beer being a strong seasonal beer first brewed in Germany. In recent years the Köbánya brewery has revived the Dreher name, and Bak is being brewed again.

# Posters - featuring brewery buildings

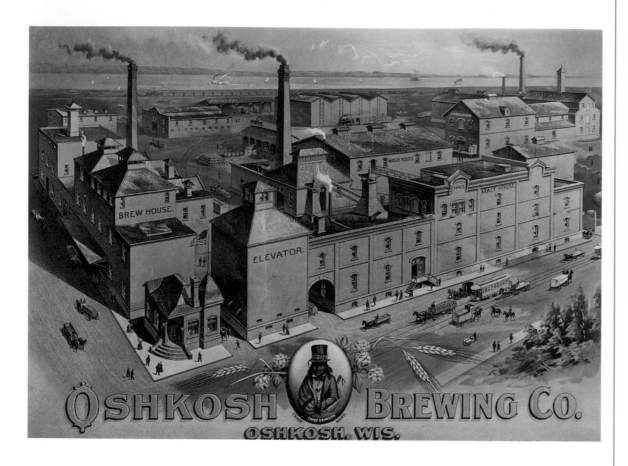

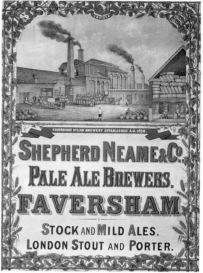

**Above** Brewers are always proud of their breweries, and this reproduction nineteenth-century poster is a typical example of the 'show-the-works' style of advertising, with smoking chimneys and cask-filled yards at the Kentish brewery of Shepherd Neame, Britain's oldest surviving beer maker.

**Above** Chief Oshkosh looks rather sourer on this pre-Prohibition brewery poster than he does on some later examples from the brewery.

**Right** A poster first printed soon after 1900, when the Hook Norton Brewery Co. Ltd of Oxfordshire, England, was launched, proudly displaying its newly rebuilt 'tower' brewery, constructed on the most modern principles (for the time) and designed by the celebrated Victorian brewery architect William Bradford.

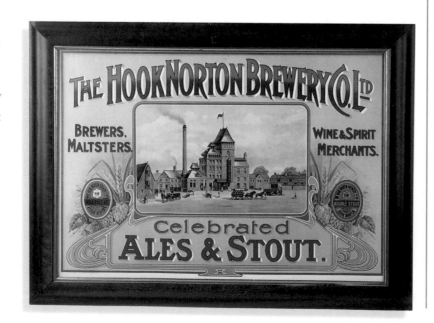

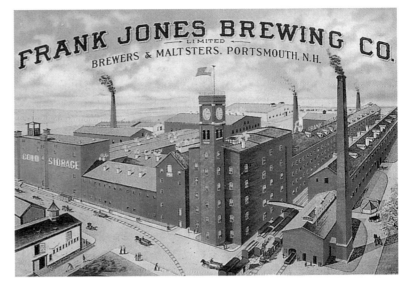

**Above** The 'busy brewery premises' theme makes an appearance in an early twentieth-century poster from the Scherdel brewery in Hof, Bavaria.

**Above** The brewery is made to dominate its surroundings in this poster from the Frank Jones Brewing Co in Portsmouth, New Hampshire.

**Right** A stunning 1930s' poster showing the busy Croix de Lorraine brewery in Bar-le-Duc, France.

# Items - featuring beer, bottles, and cans

**Above** Nothing but the beer is featured in this pre-WWI poster from the English West Country brewery Anglo-Bavarian.

**Above** The ten-sided pint glass turns up again in an early 1950s poster from Middlesborough's brewery in Selby, West Yorkshire. The brewery stopped operating in 1954 and started again in 1972.

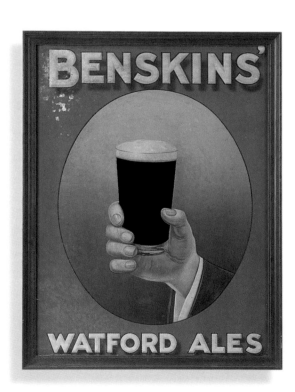

**Above** A late nineteenth-century wooden advertising sign for the Hertfordshire, England, brewer Benskin's: the 'beer glass' is actually a cut-out, with a coloured gel behind, to try to give a three-dimencional effect.

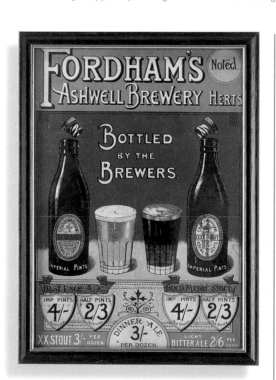

**Above** Classic early twentieth-century advertising from a little English country brewery, showing off its stoppered pint bottles.

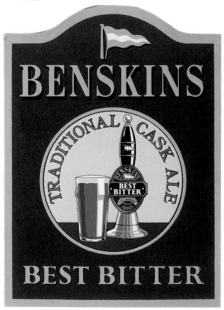

**Above** In the 1980s the revival of vanished brewery names by the big companies that had taken them over decades before saw enamel signs such as this one go up outside pubs across England's northern Home Counties, the joke being that many had never been Benskin's pubs.

Sapporo Imported Draft Beer.

**Above** In the early 1980s the British brewer Whitbread started promoting the beers from its regional breweries under their own names. The former Nimmo's brewery in the village of Castle Eden, Durham (now independent again after a management buy-out), had a very attractive poster designed for it.

**Below** A simple cardboard point-of-sale display card for Belgium's Stella Artois with a slogan that must mean more in the original Flemish than it seems to in translation.

**Top** A very 1980s poster from the Japanese brewery Sapporo for the English-speaking market.

**Middle** A coaster holder from the Belgian Moortgat brewery, makers of Duvel ale, of the sort common in bars throughout mainland Europe, where every customer generally gets a personal beermat.

**Bottom** Like many brewers, Adnam's of Southwold, on the English east coast, had to boast of the awards its beer had won in this point-of-sale card from the late 1930s for Nut Brown Ale.

# Items - featuring beer and bottles

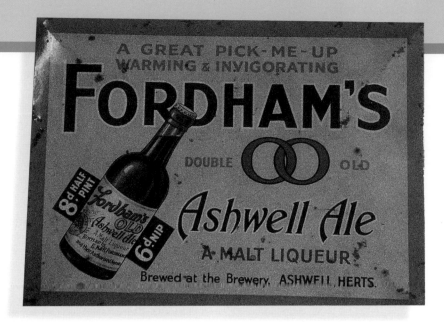

**Above** This advertisement comes from between 1888, when Wehr-Hobelmann-Gottlieb adopted the name Globe Brewery, and March 1899, when the brewery merged with 16 other local concerns to form the Maryland Brewing Co. Inc., later Gottlieb-Bauernschmidt-Straus.

**Above** A tin on card hanging advertisement from 1930s Britain for a strong bottled ale – 8d or eight pence for a half pint was four times the price of ordinary draft beer.

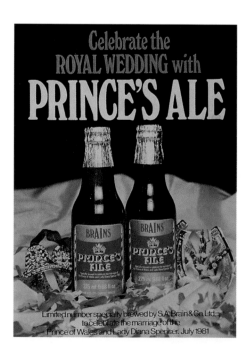

**Above** A rare example of point-of-sale material for a one-off beer, by the Welsh brewer Brains for its Royal Wedding ale of 1981.

**Above** An old enamel ad for Suffolk in England's Adnams Brewery.

**Below** An American microbrewers' 'tent,' from California's Hubsch brewpub in Davis.

# Items - featuring logos and slogans

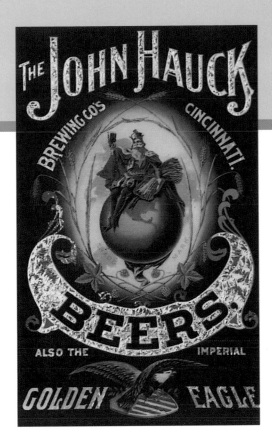

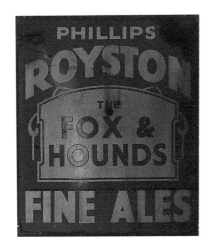

**Above** An enameled sign from the Oshkosh Brewing Company from the Wisconsin town of the same name, showing its Chief Oshkosh logo. The brewery closed in 1971 after 107 years of operation.

**Above** An enamel inn sign from 1940s Britain, with the Brewer's home town bigger than the pub name.

**Below** A modern metal wall sign for one of Britain's biggest-selling draft ales.

**Above** A glass saloon bar sign from John Hauck Brewing of Cincinnati, which closed in 1919. It was one of a large number of American brewers to use Gambrinus, the legendary 'King of Beer,' on its advertising.

**Above** Arkells brewery is in the English railway town of Swindon, so this metal pub sign is made in the style of a locomotive name plate.

**Below** Dutch Club, advertised on this illuminated sign with its beclogged waiter, is a brand from the Pittsburgh Brewing Co of Pennsylvania.

**Left** The horse brass is a traditional decorative element in older, more rural pubs in the British Isles, though brasses issued by brewers, like this one from the Bass brewery in Belfast, are unusual.

# Items - featuring logos and slogans

**Above** A hanging wall sign for the Jung Brewing Co. of Cherry Street, Milwaukee, founded in 1896 by the former brewmaster at what became Pabst's brewery.

**Above** This beautiful curved sign for John G Geyer's Cass River brewery of Frankenmuth, Michigan, was designed to go up at the entrance to the bar. The brewery was founded in 1862 and acquired by John Geyer in 1874. His grandson, Walter, retired as brewmaster only in 1983.

**Above** The rhinestone bar boy – a pre-Prohibition reverse-on-glass sign from Chattanooga Brewing – is set in a zinc frame decorated with rhinestones.

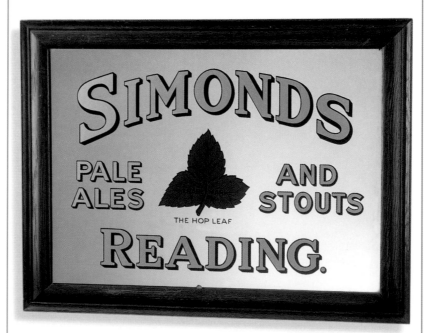

**Above** Like most pub mirrors, this example from the big Simonds brewery in Reading, Berkshire, is too crowded with letters and logo to be useful for checking that your hat is on straight.

**Above** The Dublin Brewing Company, a microbrewery in Ireland, invoked the names of a couple of early Irish girls, Maeve and Aoife (pronounced 'eefer'), to promote its draft wheat beer in 1998.

**Above** Perry's of Rathdowney, in Laois, Ireland, produced this plastic point-of-sale display shortly before it closed in 1967.

# Bottles & cans

The invention of bottled beer is generally credited to the Elizabethan Englishman Dr Alexander Nowell, who was rector of Much Hadham in Hertfordshire from 1562 and later dean of St Paul's Cathedral in London. Nowell (or Noel) was a keen fisherman, and one day, returning from a fishing session on the River Ash near Much Hadham, he 'unwittingly' left behind in the grass by the river's edge a home-corked bottle of ale he had taken with him for refreshment. When Nowell returned a few days later, the bottle was still where he had left it, and as he opened the bottle, in the words of Thomas Fuller, writing in the 1660s, he 'found it no bottle, but a gun, such the sound at the opening thereof; and this is believed (causality is the mother of more invention than industry) the origin of bottled ale in England.'

What had happened to Nowell's ale in the bottle, of course, was that a secondary fermentation had taken place, pressurizing the liquid inside with $CO_2$ gas, which accounts for the loud noise when he finally took the cork out. The advantage of bottled beer, apart from its ready portability, was that, properly sealed, it kept much longer than beer in cask. It was more expensive than cask beer, but it was popular with the aristocracy. Records of the Russell family, Earls and (later) Dukes of Bedford, show 10½ barrels of beer being purchased in 1676 from a brewer near their country seat of Woburn, Bedfordshire, 'to bottle for my lord's drinking.'

Not all experts approved of bottled beer, however. Thomas Tryon, author of one of the earliest books on brewing, *A New Art of Brewing Beere*, wrote in 1691:

'It is a great custom and general fashion nowadays to bottle ale; but the same was never invented by any true naturalist that understood the inside of things. For though ale be never so well wrought or fermented in the barrel, yet the bottling of it puts it on a new motion or fermentation, which wounds the pure spirits and ... body; therefore such ale out of bottles will drink more cold and brisk, but not so sweet and mild as the same ale out of a cask, that is of a proper age: besides the bottle tinges or gives it a cold hard quality, which is the nature of glass and stone, and being the quantity is so small, the cold Saturnine nature of the bottle has the greater power to tincture the liquor with its quality. Furthermore, all such bottle drinks are infected with a yeasty furious foaming matter which no barrel-ale is guilty of ... for which reason bottle-ale or beer is not so good or wholesome as that drawn out of the barrel or hogshead; and the chief thing that can be said for bottle-ale or beer is that it will keep longer than in barrels, which is caused by its being kept, as it were, in continued motion or fermentation.'

## THE IMPORTANCE OF BOTTLE-MAKERS

Bottled beer remained a luxury, and was generally only used for the export market, for another 150 years. Bottles themselves were expensive, and each one had to be filled and corked by hand, with the corks held down by wire. Anyone bottling beer for a long journey overseas was advised to let it go flat before corking it, since secondary fermentation in the bottle would give quite enough carbonation. Outside Europe, bottles were often scarce, and in Bristol, England, it was the bottle-makers who bottled beer for export because sending their product abroad with something saleable inside gave a double profit. In the American colonies, brewers sometimes had to advertise for empty bottles, and in 1790 the US Congress approved an $8,000 loan (a huge sum for the time) to a bottle-maker in Maryland to rebuild his factory specifically to make beer bottles.

Early bottles were hand-blown or made with primitive molds made of clay, wood, brass, and other materials which were not very suitable. A patent for iron bottle molds was granted to Joseph Magown in the United States in 1847,

Right **A half-pint bottle, probably post-World War I, from the big British brewer Whitbread.**

and in 1866 the chilled iron mold was invented, which cut costs and speeded up production. In 1835 the great London porter brewery Barclay Perkins was bottling just four percent of its output. But bottled beer now began to increase in popularity, helped in Britain by the removal of glass tax in 1845. Strangely a decline in beer consumption also helped. Where a householder would have bought a four-and-a-half gallon wooden cask to last a week, now he was happier to take a crate of four quart bottles, which kept longer in good condition.

## BOTTLES AND CORKERS

The London brewer Whitbread began one of the earliest big bottling operations in 1870. But the bottles used still had to be corked, which meant an army of workers had to be employed for this purpose. Whitbread employed more than a hundred corkers, each man working a 12-hour day, in 1886. Every bottle had to be inserted into a leather 'boot' held between the knees, and the cork knocked in with a 'flogger.' Corked beer bottles were also inconvenient for the drinker because a corkscrew was required, and bottles could not be easily resealed. A short time later, in 1873, Adolphus Busch began America's first large-scale bottling operation at the Anheuser brewery in St Louis.

In 1879 an Englishman, Henry Barrett, invented the screwtop beer bottle, a cheap, convenient, reusable container that meant little or no waste. The molds for the bottles came in three pieces, one each for the sides and one for the top. The screwtop beer bottle caught on rapidly. Even when an American, William Painter, invented the crown cork in 1892, screwtops were still used for quart bottles where the customer might want to reseal the container in order to have some more beer later. In continental Europe, however, the place of the screwtop was taken by the porcelain swing-top closure.

Bottled beer was given a further boost by the discoveries of the French scientist Louis Pasteur in the

Right **Corona and Sol may get connoisseurs of beers turning up their noses, but connoisseurs of packaging *love* their 'retro' designs.**

Far right **China's importance as a brewing nation is growing fast. This beer comes from the big Shanghai brewery.**

1870s, which led to the invention of pasteurization. Beer was heated in bottles to 122 Fahrenheit for a half hour, which killed off any bugs in the beer and left it stable and unlikely to go off for many months. Pasteur had taken an interest in brewing because he wanted to help French brewers in their fight for market share against their German rivals. The first brewery to pasteurize its beer, not surprisingly in view of Pasteur's nationality, seems to have been French, Velten of Marseilles. But the idea caught on quickly with brewers in the United States, who were subjecting their bottled beers to 'the steaming process' as early as 1877. They allied the technique with new developments in chilling, filtering, and carbonating to produce long-lasting, stable, sparkling beers.

## WHY MOST BEER BOTTLES ARE BROWN

Beer bottles are still generally brown, for a very good reason: ordinary sunlight quickly affects some of the bittering components in beer, producing an unpleasant skunklike aroma, a condition known as 'lightstruck.' Brown glass gives the best protection against light, while green glass or clear glass (known as flint glass)

give no protection at all. Some clear glass bottles are now being produced with a covering that lets normal light through but keeps ultraviolet light out, in an attempt to solve this problem.

Over the years, bottled beers came to dominate sales in most parts of the world, even after the arrival of canned beers in the mid-1930s. At the end of the twentieth century, draft beer accounted for the majority of beer sales only in the British Isles (Ireland and the UK), while bottled beer made up 67 percent of sales in Germany, 56 percent in Belgium, 57 percent in Spain, and 37 percent in the United States. In Britain and Ireland the volume of beer sold in bottles is just 10 percent or less. However, in both the United

# Bottles & cans

States and Britain the growth in the number of small or 'boutique' breweries has seen a boom in the range of bottled beers available, many featuring beer styles that were once all but vanished, including porters, oatmeal stouts, strong IPAs and the like.

Britain is also, with New Zealand, the home of the commemorative bottle. The Association of Bottled Beer Collectors estimates that a complete collection of UK commemorative bottled beers would total around 2,700 bottles. The events range from Queen Victoria's Golden Jubilee in 1887 to the Millennium, including almost 150 issued for the wedding of Prince Charles, the Prince of Wales, to Lady Diana Spencer in 1981. Other commemorative bottles have marked events such as the soccer World Cup, victory in World War II, the 350th anniversary of the departure of the Pilgrim Fathers to America, the 50th anniversary of the Easter Rising in Dublin, and national independence in countries such as Nigeria and Kenya. In New Zealand special bottlings have been made for everything from rugby club centenaries to sheepdog trials.

## BOTTLES FROM AROUND THE WORLD

Even if you do not want to collect commemoratives, however, it is easy to build up a collection of beers from all around the world: today many ordinary package stores and supermarkets carry a changing range of bottled beers from foreign countries, while specialist beer shops will have beers you have never heard of from countries you might not have heard of, either. These are sold more to please the beer drinker than the collector, but the rise in interest in bottled beers does mean it is probably easier for the bottled beer collector to build up a display of unusual and attractive items more quickly and less expensively than any other beer memorabilia fan.

Older and rarer items turn up in unexpected places: junk and secondhand stores sometimes have odd bottles, still full, that might be 50 years old or more, and collectors' fairs will generally have several stalls where you can find full bottles. If your interest is in older embossed bottles, flea markets, collectors' fairs, and secondhand

Right **An American example from the Latrobe brewery of Pennsylvania which produces Rolling Rock.**

shops are often full of these. Old bottles sometimes turn up at auction houses, too, though they normally fetch prices that make ordinary collectors suck their teeth in dismay. A full bottle of King's Ale, brewed by Bass of Burton-upon-Trent in 1902, sold at auction a few years back for the pound sterling equivalent of $400. The same beer could be found at a collectors' fair in Britain for a tenth of that price.

Bottles are generally regarded as more collectable if they still contain the beer, although this gives the bottle collector a problem: full bottles weigh a lot. If you want to display your collection, you will require strong shelves firmly attached to the walls, or a sturdy, well-made cabinet. One problem is that bottle tops, especially on older bottles, have a tendency to rust. A coat of clear lacquer over the bottle top may solve this problem. Some collectors have tried sealing wax, but this is generally felt to ruin the look. If you have to store your bottles away in boxes, protect the label with plastic wrap and make sure your storage place is dry and not prone to condensation, because labels on bottles can easily go moldy.

## BEER CANS

It took more than a century from the first use of tin cans for storing food to their successful launch as beer containers. The metal can was invented in 1810, and the earliest food canning factory opened in London around 1812. But to begin with, tin cans were popular only with the British Royal Navy and polar explorers, who were using them in the 1830s on long voyages in order to keep food fresh.

Food canning started in America around 1837, as glass jars became too costly to use for many food items, and canning really took off during the American Civil War. (The world had to wait another two decades for Ezra Warner of Waterbury, Connecticut, to invent the can opener in 1858, incidentally. Before Warner, using a hammer and chisel was the quickest way into the tin.) By the 1880s factories in America were canning fish, fruit, vegetables, corned beef, and milk.

Beer was occasionally taken home from the bar or public house in tin containers. There was a good trade in specially shaped tin flasks in Wales after a Sunday closing law was passed in 1881. Publicans would supply the flasks, which were designed to fit closely to the body under the clothes, so that customers could sneak beer away from the pub on a Sunday in their tin 'belly cans' for a drink at home. But the beer stayed only a short time in the tin, and outside Wales, glass bottles or stoneware jars remained supreme for taking beer home.

The first known attempt at the commercial canning of beer came in 1909, when the American Can Company experimented with beer cans at the request of a brewer in Montana. They were not a success, however, because the beer reacted with the inside of the can to produce an unacceptable 'tinny' flavor. Then Prohibition put an end to any further ideas of canning beer, and it was not until 1931, when it looked hopeful that beer drinking might soon be legalized again in the United States, that the American Can Company looked once more at the possibilities. After two years, the company had developed a plastic inner coating for the cans that would protect the beer from the metal. By this time Prohibition had been repealed, but the American Can Company was unable to find a big brewer willing to try out its beer in tins. Anheuser-Busch and Pabst had both, apparently, tried canning beer in 1929 and had decided the product was not yet good enough.

The first brewer who would participate in the experiment was the Gottfried Krueger Brewing Company of Newark, New Jersey. Krueger was struggling to make a profit, and had been hit by a workers' strike soon after Prohibition ended. The American Can Company offered to install the canning line free, with Krueger only paying if the beer was successful. Two thousand cans were filled in a trial run in 1933. Drinkers liked it: more than 90 percent of those who tried the new beer gave their

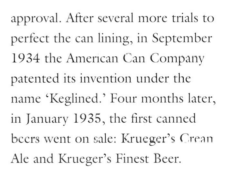

Right **Like other breweries, Mansfield Brewery in the Midlands produced a commemorative ale and sold its bottled Millennium ale in this attractive tin container.**

approval. After several more trials to perfect the can lining, in September 1934 the American Can Company patented its invention under the name 'Keglined.' Four months later, in January 1935, the first canned beers went on sale: Krueger's Cream Ale and Krueger's Finest Beer.

## THE CONVENIENCE OF CANS

Within six months, Krueger's output was running at more than five times its precanning levels. American shoppers loved the new containers: they were lighter to carry home, and they fitted more easily into the refrigerators that increasing numbers of American homes possessed. Other brewers were forced to follow Krueger's lead. By the end of 1935, 37 American breweries had started selling canned beer, including Pabst, which rattled out its first cans in July, just six months after Krueger, and Schlitz, which produced its first cans in September.

The American Can Company's beer cans were the type known as 'flat tops,' which needed a special opener (also made by the company) to pierce the tops. In September 1935 its rival, the Continental Can Company, introduced the 'cone top,' which was sealed with a crown cork just like those used on bottled beers. The first brewer to use cone top cans was the G Heilemann Brewing Co. of La Crosse, Wisconsin. The advantage to brewers, particularly the smaller ones, was that they could use at least some of their old bottling plant to fill and seal these cans. The disadvantage to the consumer was that they did not stack as well in the refrigerator as flat-top cans did. They also bore an unfortunate

# Bottles & cans

similarity to the cans used for metal polish. Even so, cone-top cans were on sale in the United States until 1965. The brewers were sometimes lyrical in promoting their use. For example the Duquesne Brewing Company of Pittsburgh, which first produced its 'Can-o-Beer' in 1935, wrote on the back of the can: 'This cap-sealed can brings Duquesne Beer to you with its outstandingly fine flavor unimpaired. Light cannot affect it. It visits no home but yours. It cools quickly, and takes up little space. Open it like a bottle – drink from it if you wish. When emptied, crush it and throw it away. No empties to return. No "extras" for deposits.'

The French like to claim the credit for the first canned beer in Europe, giving the honors to a brewery called Moreau and Company in Vezelize, Lorraine, in 1933. Moreau, which used flat-top cans, advertised its 'bières en boîtes' as 'Le Goût du Jour' ('The Taste of Today.') Despite this early start, however, canned beer still only represents five percent of French beer sales.

## INITIAL SKEPTICISM

In Britain, brewers were deeply skeptical about the idea of canning beer. Sanders Watney of the London brewery company Watney Combe Reid (he was later known for driving Watney's stagecoach, the Red Rover) said in 1934, 'I am not convinced that there would be any demand for beer in cans. I cannot conceive the idea of a can ever replacing the half-pint, pint, or quart bottle. The canning habit is certainly growing, but I do not think it will spread to drinks.' Ironically, Watney's brewery was later one of the biggest promoters of beer in cans, especially in large sizes…but, as in America, it took a small brewer to blaze the technological trail.

The little Welsh brewery of Felinfoel (pronounced vell-in-voe-ell), near Llanelli, was owned by the John family, who also had a financial interest in the St David's tinplate works a couple of miles from the brewery. South Wales was still suffering badly from the Depression, and tinplate manufacturers were hugely interested in the explosion in tinplate production that the introduction of canned beer had brought in America. For the Johns, canned beer

Right **Germany's first beer can was this cone top for 'export' bier.**

perfectly combined their two businesses. An approach was made to Metal Box, Britain's biggest can manufacturer, which, despite its doubts, agreed to test the idea of making canned beer. Late in 1935 a manufacturing line was erected at a factory in Acton, west London, with the St David's works supplying the tinplate. The cans were then taken to south Wales for the Felinfoel brewery to fill them with beer. These were cone-top cans, filled with a half pint each of pale ale and sealed with a crown cork. The lining, developed by Metal Box, was an undercoat of lacquer with a topping of wax. The Welsh brewers were proud that, unlike the American version, their cans were filled with unpasteurized beer. Felinfoel's head brewer, Sidney John, declared: 'The difficulties of the London Metal Box Company have been to find a lining to preserve beer in its best state. After considerable research work, they have succeeded in doing so – the Americans have not.' Every brewery employee, and every worker at the St David's tinplate plant, was given a can of the beer to mark this Welsh triumph. The cans are, today, rare and valuable.

The next brewer in Britain to can beer, and the first to can lager, was Jeffreys of Edinburgh. It was followed by two London brewers, Barclay Perkins and Hammertons. Other brewers with a big export sale, Simonds of Reading, McEwan's of Edinburgh, and Tennents of Glasgow, joined the bandwagon. By the fall of 1937, 23 British breweries were making canned beer. Among the beers that had appeared was a special canned ale from the Felinfoel brewery for the coronation of King George VI in May that year.

However, there were problems. Despite Sidney John's boasts, the lining invented by Metal Box did spoil the taste of the beer. Returnable bottles cost no more than cans, and could be reused an average of 200 times. When World War II came, most brewers in Britain were banned from using cans except for beer destined for the troops. Only Felinfoel, because of its links with the tinplate industry, was allowed to sell canned beer in Britain.

### CAMOUFLAGED CANS

In America, too, canned beer was restricted to the troops, at home and overseas. Some cans were even painted in 'olive drab' to camouflage them from enemy snipers. After the war cans became anything but drab. The nature of cans meant they could be made much more visually striking than bottles. Cans were growing larger, with the introduction of the 16-ounce can by Schlitz in 1954, and lighter, with aluminum being used for beer cans by Coors in 1959. The ring-pull can was developed by the Iron City Brewery Company of Pittsburgh, Pennsylvania, in 1962, sparking a boom in can sales. By 1969 canned beer was outselling bottled beer in the United States for the first time.

The ring-pull can crossed the Atlantic in 1964, and had a similar effect on the battle between glass and metal to the one it had in America. In Britain, bottles fell from 94 percent of packaged beer sales in 1968 to 16 percent in 1979, with 78 percent sold in cans. However, few countries outside the United States have such a deep love of the beer can. Canned beer still has around 53 percent of sales in the United States; only Sweden matches this in Europe, with some 58 percent of beer sold in cans. In most other European countries cans make up just five to 15 percent of the market, with Britain halfway between Europe and America at 24 percent. Even the invention by Guinness in 1989 of the 'widget' can, which contains a small plastic device inside that gives a head on the beer closer to the one found on draft beer when it is poured out, failed to knock 'genuine' draft beer from its pole position in Britain and Ireland. In Denmark, no cans of beer are sold at all; everything has to be in returnable bottles.

Left **This collectible variation on the Newcastle Brown Ale can comes in the black-and-white stripes of the Newcastle United soccer club in England.**

### THE BEER CAN COLLECTORS OF AMERICA

Not surprisingly, the popularity of beer can collecting in different countries matches up with the popularity of canned beer. In the United States it is one of the biggest areas of beer memorabilia, with a thriving society devoted to the hobby – the Beer Can Collectors of America. In Europe, only the Swedes seem to collect beer cans to any great extent. Britain has a tiny number of can collectors, compared to those who collect coasters, bottles, or labels. Even so, the biggest collection in the United Kingdom numbers some 18,000 cans.

New cans are easy to get hold of, but older ones are harder to find; after all, these were items designed to be thrown away. They do turn up at flea markets, collectors' fairs, garage sales, and the like, however, and except for the rarer pre-World War II examples, prices are normally very reasonable. Like most beer memorabilia areas, however, probably the best way to acquire older cans is through a collectors' club or association.

Whether you should collect your cans full or empty is a matter of choice, but most collectors seem to prefer their cans empty. The cans are, of course, much lighter that way, and it avoids any problems with older cans rusting or leaking. However, the best way to open a can you want to display is through the underside, rather than the top, so that the inevitable hole is hidden. Make two holes in the bottom of the can, to let the beer flow out more easily, using a wooden-handled awl – and do it in the sink or in a bucket to avoid making a mess with the inevitable jet of pressurized beer.

Displaying your cans is, again, a matter of choice. Most collectors put their cans up on shelves; only a few have special cabinets made. The Beer Can Collectors of America sells a cardboard 'can tote' for $8 which will accommodate most every size of can from cone-top to 500ml 'sta-tab,' and holds up to 48 cans. If, however, you are aiming for a collection of 18,000 cans, you will need a lot of totes!

# Old bottles

**Below** A stoneware ginger beer bottle from a brewer in southern England. This rare type from Christie's of Hoddesdon was designed to be used closed with a crown cork.

**Above** Two late nineteenth-century embossed bottles from Chattanooga Brewing of Tennessee.

**Below** A line-up of empty bottles from Hamm's brewery of St Paul, Minnesota. Zumalweiss, on the end, was a 'near beer' made during the years of Prohibition.

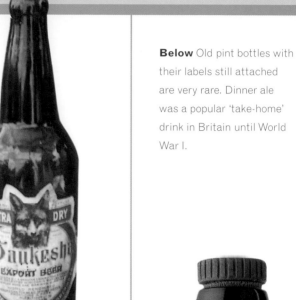

**Above** Water for the Waukesha Brewing Company's beers came in part from the Fox Head spring in Waukesha, Wisconsin, and the Fox Head became the company trademark. During Prohibition the company name was changed to Fox Head.

**Below** Old pint bottles with their labels still attached are very rare. Dinner ale was a popular 'take-home' drink in Britain until World War I.

48

# Old & dated bottles

**Below** It is good to get an ad display still with its original bottle. Fitger's of Duluth, Minnesota, which closed in 1972, was not the only American brewery to sell beer called Rex – the other was Maier, in Los Angeles – but it could boast: 'Brewed on the shores of Lake Superior.'

**Right** A rare full clear-glass bottle from Kolb's brewery in Bay City, Michigan.

**Below** A 1997-dated 'harvest ale,' from JW Lees of Manchester, in the northwest of England.

**Right** Bottles in three different sizes from the now-closed Gluek's of Minneapolis, which started life around 1859.

**Left** A line-up of early bottles from Minneapolis Brewing, which changed its company name to that of its well-known trademark, Grain Belt, in 1967 and closed nine years later. Like Hamm's, it once brewed a beer called Zumalweiss.

Only a few brewers used to put 'vintage dates' on their (very strongest) beers, generally on those bottles that would improve over five or ten years or more. But the habit is growing now for 'harvest' bottled beers brewed with the first malt and hops of the season, which normally need drinking quickly, like a nouveau wine, and do not improve with keeping – though that makes them not a whit less collectable …

**Below** The supreme example of a 'vintage' English strong bottled beer is Thomas Hardy's Ale, from the Eldridge Pope brewery in Dorset, and named for the English novelist. It has been brewed almost every year since 1968, and is supposed to have a shelflife of up to 25 years. The two examples here are from 1975 (which makes it more than ready for drinking!) and the 'Silver Anniversary' bottle of 1993, which celebrated 25 years of Thomas Hardy's Ale.

**Below** An example of a classic beer, Imperial Russian Stout, brewed by the British company Courage. This 1975 version was made at the original Courage brewery by Tower Bridge in London, closed in 1981.

**Above** The Trappist monks of Chimay (more properly L'Abbaye de Notre Dame de Scourmont at Forges-les-Chimay, Hainault, Belgium) bottle their strong 'Chimay Bleu' in 75cl (25 US fl oz) dated, corked bottles under the name Grand Reserve. The illustrated example is from 1992.

Around the time of World War II many brewers in Britain began using 'fired-on' or silk-screen labels on their bottles, partly because shortages of paper meant normal labels were not available. Most are just one color, but even these are often attractive and collectable.

**Below** A half-pint bottle from England, the traditional style from the Bristol brewery George & Co.

**Below and right** Two screwtop fired-on bottles from small English brewers where the idea of the design is to look like a label without being specific about the precise brand inside.

**Above** The Scottish brewer MacLachlans faithfully reproduced its paper labels for Castle Ale in fired-on form, including the, 'This label is issued by ...' statement around the edge.

# Modern bottles

**Below** Europe's biggest user of fired-on labels is Belgium. Here are an 'abbey' beer brewed by commercial brewers; and Rochefort, a genuine Trappist abbey brew.

**Below** The Scottish brewer Belhaven tried a fired-on label for an attempt on the American market with this pint bottle in the early 1980s.

**Above right** An early 1990s fired-on bottle from the Danish brewer Carlsberg for the English-speaking markets.

**Above left** An Asian fired-on label, from San Miguel in the Philippines.

The use of fired on bottle labels by Mexican brewers was originally part of their cheap and cheerful approach to the product. It meant the bottles could be reused without the expense of washing off the old paper labels or relabeling them when they were filled. The success of Corona (now the biggest-selling imported beer in the United States) and Sol in import markets means that fired-on labels have become almost a necessity for the credibility of beers from the general Caribbean area in export markets, as this selection shows.

**Below** This lovely label is carried by bottles from Impala Breweries of Goa in India. The back label carries the instruction, 'For real fun, drink chilled.'

**Above left** Keo, from the town of Lemesos in southern Cyprus, is one of the last independent breweries to be found in the Greek-speaking world.

**Above right** Dos Equis, or 'two crosses,' from the Moctezuma brewery company in Mexico, is a darkish lager showing the Viennese influence on the country's brewing styles.

**Below right** The best-known beer in South Africa is Castle lager, from South African Breweries.

**Below center** White Cap was originally made by a brewery called Allsopp, East Africa which merged with Kenya Breweries in 1962, and which still makes the beer today.

**Below left** Jamaica's Dragon stout represents the Caribbean's fondness for strong, sweet, black beers.

# Anniversary & Christmas bottles

**Below** A rare full bottle of silver jubilee beer celebrating the 25-year reign of King George V in 1935 from the Burton-upon-Trent brewer Ind Coope & Allsopp in England. The firm was a merger between two big Burton breweries that had taken place only the previous year.

**Above** A trio of full bottles of strong ale from British brewers celebrating Queen Elizabeth II's silver jubilee in 1977, from Ind Coope of Essex and Burton, Hook Norton of Oxfordshire and Shepherd Neame of Kent.

**Below** Two bottles from the coronation of Queen Elizabeth II in 1953 from brewers in Hertfordshire, England.

**Above** The Millennium celebrations naturally needed their own special beers. This English pair came from King and Barnes in Sussex and the Old Chimneys brewery in Suffolk, which printed the label of its Two Thousand Year Ale in the English of a thousand years ago.

Anniversaries and special events of all sorts spur brewers into producing special beers, though at first they were draft beers only. In 1737, when the Prince of Wales's baby daughter was born, he had barrels of beer brewed by the east London brewer Truman's put outside his home in London, Carlton House, for Londoners to toast the birth. Special Christmas beers, often spiced and generally strong, have been made since at least the nineteenth century, and their labels are frequently colorful and collectable.

**Below** Make your own beer memorabilia! London and Dublin Stout was commissioned by the author in 1997 from the Pitfield Brewery on the edge of the City of London to celebrate his marriage to a lass from Dublin.

**Below** Often a brewery will celebrate an event in the family with a special beer. The Traquair House brewery in Scotland brought out this brew for the silver wedding anniversary of its owner, who is the Laird of Traquair, Peter Maxwell Stuart, and his wife.

**Below** Two of the series of Christmas beers made by the Anchor brewery in San Francisco since 1974, each one with a different fir tree on the label and a different recipe inside. One is a 'giant' version of the twentieth anniversary beer from 1994, holding more than three pints, the other the 1980 version.

# Christmas bottles & early cans

**Left and right** Many Belgian brewers make their own Christmas beers: these two are from the Duboisson brewery in Hainault, and the Dolle Brouwers in Esens, West Flanders.

**Above** The Norwegian brewer Frydenlund features Scandinavian-style candles on its attractive Juleøl (Christmas ale) label.

**Right** A very unusual Christmas beer was made by the Burton Bridge brewery in Burton-upon-Trent, England, for a local firm, and bottled in stoneware jars.

**Left** A rare Christmas lager from the Danish giant Carlsberg, issued in 1994.

**Right** In the early 1980s Guinness produced small amounts of a special strong Christmas brew, supposedly by Father Guinness Son and Co., with a jokey interpretation of the traditional Guinness label.

There are an estimated 5,400 breweries in operation around the world right now, in more than 150 countries, and with breweries opening and closing every week it would be an almost imposible task to collect an example from every brewery that bottled beer, everywhere. But you might just try to see how many different countries you could collect beers from. Here is a tiny selection from five continents of what is available, to bring on your collecting thirst.

**Left** The Sailer brewery in Marktoberdorf, Bavaria, Germany sells a porcelain-stoppered Weinachtsbier showing Santa's sleigh loaded with beers.

## THE KELLOGG KRUEGER COLLECTION

Cans from the pioneer of canned beer in America, G. Krueger of Newark, New Jersey, with the 'K' man trademark prominent. Three giant die-cut steel K-men were positioned on top of the brewery's 11-story grain elevator in Newark. It closed in 1960 and was demolished in 1986. This sign advertising the cans, and the cans themselves, come from the fine Krueger Collection of Elaine Kellogg of Kalamazoo, Michigan.

**Right** Another California Christmas ale, from North Coast Brewing in Fort Bragg, dated 1989, just two years after the brewery started out.

# Cans - old

**Below** Duquesne's 'Can-o-Beer' cone-top can from 1935, worth more than five times as much as its contemporary the Budweiser can, only partly because of the comparative rarity of cone-tops. As a regional brewer its production was smaller anyway, making surviving cans rarer, and it is also a more attractive can. The company, which sold its first beer in 1900, closed in 1972.

**Above** An early cone-top can from the Felinfoel brewery in south Wales, the pioneer of beer canning in Britain.

**Above** One of the rarest cans in the world, issued for the coronation of King George VI in 1937 by Simonds' brewery in Reading, England.

**Above** Water for the Waukesha Brewing Company's beers came in part from the Fox Head spring in Waukesha, Wisconsin, and the Fox Head became the company trademark. During Prohibition the company name was changed to Fox Head. The brewery was taken over and closed by G. Heilemann of LaCrosse, Wisconsin in 1962, although the brand lived on.

**Below** Not strictly a beer can, but still very collectable, this is the sort of business American brewers had to get into during the long years of Prohibition.

**Above** Brew 77 was introduced by the William Gerst Brewing Co. of Nashville, Tennessee, in 1953, only a year before it closed.

**Above** An early 'flat-top' Budweiser can in unfamiliar colors from the 1930s, issued by Anheuser-Busch with instructions on the side on how to open the can with the Canco 'quick and easy' opener.

**Below** An early ring-pull can of Laurentide beer from Molson's Quebec brewery.

A selection of cans with Kentucky Derby themes, from Sterling of Evansville, Indiana, Fehr of Louisville, Kentucky, the Falstaff Corporation, and Schoenling of Cincinnati, Ohio.

**Above** A ring-pull can from the Japanese brewer Kirin, issued in the 1960s.

**Below** An English flat-top can from the early 1960s, just after the London brewers Courage and Barclay had merged with Simonds of Reading, Berkshire, England.

# Modern cans

**Above** A 'nip-size' small can for Gold Label, the strong barley wine, still brewed by the British brewer Whitbread.

**Above** A name once familiar to thousands of American servicemen, BGI ('Brasseries et Glacières de l'Indochine') of Da Nang, Vietnam, provides an example of the international possibilities of can collecting.

**Above** Brewers sometimes, as here, produce special cans to mark the opening of a new canning line, often giving the beers away to employees.

**Below** China is becoming increasingly important as a brewing nation, and cans from Chinese breweries like this one in Hangzhou, near Shanghai, are turning up in can collections.

**Above** This special-edition Sapporo can, which came out one winter in the late 1980s, is etched with little snowflakes.

**Below** Both sides of the commemorative can issued by the Welsh brewer Felinfoel for the wedding of Charles, Prince of Wales, and Lady Diana Spencer in 1981.

**Right and below** Three cans from Hawaii showing the Primo brand in different dress.

Miller HIGH LIFE Münchener STYLE
CONTENTS 12 FLUID OZ
MILWAUKEE BEER
INTERNAL REVENUE TAX PAID
BREWED & BOTTLED BY
MILLER BREWING CO.
MILWAUKEE, WIS. U.S.A.
WISC. REG. NO. B-2

# Labels & tops

The beer bottle label is considerably younger than the bottle itself. When bottled beer was still a luxury, the only maker's identification would be a wax seal imprinted with the brewer's name, or, early in the nineteenth century, the lead foil capsule still found on the more expensive sort of wine bottle. However, as the trade in bottled beers expanded, a cheaper method of branding the beer was needed. The earliest paper labels, which appeared at the beginning of the 1840s, were circular, plain black and white, and were effectively printed versions of the wax seals they were replacing. Soon afterwards a more suitable shape for mechanical application to a curved bottle came into existence: the oval label was born.

At the same time, brewers with a reputation to protect began designing more elaborate labels, to try to prevent unscrupulous rival brewers passing off inferior brews as the better-quality product. Among the very first brewers to do this was Bass of Burton-upon-Trent, in England. It was issuing bottle labels showing a red triangle surrounded by Staffordshire knots in the early 1850s. Bass's beer was one of the first with a world-renowned name. A bottle of Bass India Pale Ale can be spotted in the famous nineteenth-century painting by the French artist Édouard Manet of *The Bar at the Folies Bergère* in Paris. Even with the more complex label design, there were reports of forgeries of Bass labels from Rio de Janeiro to Hong Kong. When a law to protect trademarks was enacted in Britain in 1876, Bass's red triangle was the first to be registered.

The same year Guinness registered its brown label with the harp design. The Irish company was scrupulous in issuing its trademark

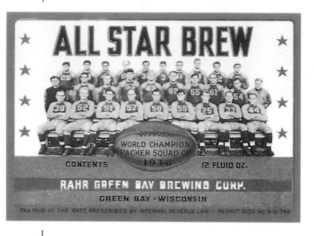

Left **A commemorative beer label from the mid-1930s, when the local brewer in Green Bay, Wisconsin, wamted to show its pride in the winning exploits of the Packers squad.**

label only to bottlers who, to quote the wording on the label, 'sell no other brown stout in bottle.' Anyone else could bottle Guinness, but they could not put the harp on the label. Anyone found using fake Guinness labels on bottles that did not contain genuine Dublin-brewed stout had to agree to sign a prepared letter of apology or face prosecution:

'I beg you to forgo legal proceedings and accept my full and most ample apology for having used your registered trademark and label in bottling stout which was not manufactured by you, and was inferior to yours; and I deeply regret having committed so great an error on my part and injustice to yours. I promise that I will never use your label in bottling stout manufactured by any other party, and you are at liberty to publish this apology in any way you may consider necessary...'

However, such threats had little effect on brewers overseas. When a partner in Tennent's brewery, Glasgow, visited Argentina to look for sales in 1875, he was unnerved to find a local brewer in Buenos Aires with a large chest full of fake Bass and Tennent bottle labels, which he 'frankly admitted' were used on the Buenos Aires brewery's bottled beers.

### THE BIRTH OF CLASSIC TRADEMARKS

In the United States the growing national brewers were also starting to use easily recognized trademarks that would appear on their beer labels. The Ballantine brewery in Newark, New Jersey, picked the three interlocking rings as its logo in 1879. Anheuser-Busch's 'A and Eagle' is said to date from 1872 and the first label for its Budweiser brand,

Right **Many brewers in Britain issued special beers when the future Queen Elizabeth II married Prince Philip, the Duke of Edinburgh, in 1947, including Warwicks & Richardsons, which ran until 1966.**

launched in 1876, is remarkably like the label still used today. The importance of brand names was recognized early by America's brewers. For example in 1886 a brewery concern in San Antonio bought the rights to Pearl beer from the Kaiser-Beck brewery in Germany. It turned out to be such a good move that they changed their name to Pearl.

Bottled beer took off in the 1880s and 1890s, a time regarded by many as the start of the 'golden age' of label design, when the purity of the design was unsullied by the need to print tax paid statements, minimum contents, best before dates, and bar codes on the labels. Hundreds of small brewers installed their first bottling lines and slapped on their first beer labels during this period. Today these labels are almost impossible to find outside other people's collections, but their style and vivacity is unsurpassed. Sometimes only single examples of labels are known from a brewery that closed 80 or 90 years ago.

The introduction of Prohibition in the United States meant that for 13 years only near beers and nonalcoholic drinks were bottled by the companies that had once been America's brewers. Labels from near-beer bottles – such as Anheuser-Busch's Bevo and Pabst's Pablo – are still collectable, but they fail to elicit the excitement that real beer labels do. In the rest of the world (except for Finland, which went 'dry' for exactly the same length of time as the United States) bottle labels continued to flourish. Germany and The Netherlands specialized in the stopper label, which acted as a guarantee that the contents had not been tampered with. Often this type of label was the only one the bottle bore. In the

United Kingdom, after 1901, screwtop bottles, which were often collected from the pub or package store by children, had by law to have a paper seal over the stopper. Generally they bore messages, such as 'Observe that this label is unbroken.'

World War II meant paper shortages, as well as serious reductions in supplies of every other raw material, and brewers did their bit by either reducing the size of their bottle labels or leaving them off entirely. Sometimes only the color of the crown cork identified the beer inside the bottle, while several brewers introduced 'permanent' fired-on or stenciled labels.

### THE MOST INTERNATIONAL OF HOBBIES

After the war the rectangular label began to dominate (though labels have been produced in almost every shape imaginable, from diamond to figure-eight). New printing techniques meant foil labels started to appear, bottled beer's answer, perhaps, to the shiny and often striking beer can. From the late 1970s in the United States, the microbrewery boom saw a huge rise in the number of modern collectable beer labels as small concerns issued a range of new beers. British microbrewers were slower at bottling their beers, since they preferred to tackle the much larger draft market, but the supermarkets have encouraged new small brewers in Britain to start bottling their products with labels and some very attractive ones have been designed. In countries such as Australia and New Zealand, new brewers have also been choosing to bottle their beers and have designed some beautiful labels.

Label collecting is one of the most international of hobbies, with collectors – especially the battalions to be found in Eastern Europe – able to amass examples from all over the world. Even 40 years ago, one famous American collector, PA Miller of Milwaukee, Wisconsin, had accumulated more than 125,000 different labels from around the globe. Perhaps the oldest breweriana collectors' organization is the Labologists' Society, founded in Britain in 1958. It is still thriving today and has its own regular newsletter. Other societies for

# Labels & tops

collectors of labels exist in the United States, Australia, New Zealand, Scandinavia, Germany, and elsewhere. Joining a collectors' society is one of the best ways to expand your collection, not only because fellow enthusiasts will be eager to swap their spare labels for yours, but because the societies will have the contacts with breweries that you might find hard to make independently. They will also hold swaps meetings and auctions, and their publications will carry small ads of labels for sale.

Although removing the label from a bottle that you bought in a bar or store is often the only way to add that example to your collection, getting a pristine version straight from the brewery is a lot better. Big brewers will be used to receiving requests from collectors for labels (and your local society will have lists of brewery addresses), but smaller brewers are often too busy to oblige. Even turning up at the brewery door (which is how many early collectors started out) may not work. In that case, make do with soaked-off labels. They are better than nothing!

Labels do occasionally turn up at collectors' fairs, flea markets, and junk shops, and you can sometimes find them by advertising in your local paper. But always beware of fakes. A number of people have bought what they thought were old labels which turned out to be color photocopies. If your local bar has a display of framed old beer labels on the wall, take a hard, close look at them. They are very likely to be photocopies, the giveaway being slight variations in areas of what should be flat color, and 'white' areas that are not quite white. Once you learn to recognize photocopies, they should be easy to pick out.

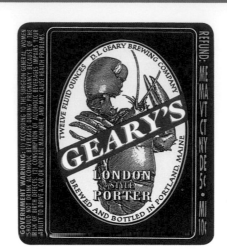

Left **A more modern American porter, from D.L. Geary Brewing of Portland, Maine, a microbrewery that started in 1986, when it was the first commercial brewery in the state for a century.**

Right **A label on a bottle on a label from another Scottish brewer, Calder's of Alloa.**

Left **Sometimes old labels such as this Christmas Ale one from the Scottish brewer McEwan's will turn up at an auction, or even a swapmeet.**

Most collectors will specialize in a specific area of label collecting: their own country, a particular region or town, a particular era. Like foreign stamps, however, beer labels from faraway lands have a fascinating exoticism; a label from the Falkland Islands' only brewery seems intrinsically more collectable than a Bud label.

## REMOVING LABELS

If removing a label from a bottle is the only option, older labels can be soaked off with very hot water and a (not too sharp) razor blade – but take great care (and do not try this unsupervised if you are under 16). The bottle should be placed in nearly boiling water for up to 20 seconds to soften the glue, taken out (hold it with a towel to avoid burning yourself), and the razor blade inserted under the edge and worked around the label. Dip the bottle back in the hot water to continue softening the glue, take it slowly, and be careful. It is best to practice your technique on nonvital labels first. When the label is fully removed, scrape off any remaining glue from the back and dry it carefully by pressing it on a flat surface between two towels. The still-damp label can be laid on blotting paper (perhaps with wax paper behind it) and then weighted down for as long as 48 hours to dry out flat.

Self-adhesive labels can also be removed by placing the bottle in a hot oven 400 degrees Fahrenheit for five to ten minutes. Again, be very careful when removing the bottle and peeling off the label, that you do not burn yourself. A razor blade inserted under one corner of the label will start the removal process. Stick the removed label to a new sheet of paper and either insert that into your album or trim round it and mount it as usual.

However that does not answer the most difficult question for serious label collectors: how to store and display your labels safely. Paper labels were never designed to last ten or more years, and they will fade slowly if kept in the light, while the paper is likely to turn brown (so framing real labels and hanging them on the wall is a very bad idea). Even in the dark, however, the glues you use to adhere the labels to the pages of your binder or album, and the acids in the plastic and paper used to make the album, can cause long-term damage, fading, and staining.

The British collector Mike Jones recommends avoiding all plastics (acid-free plastic is available, but it is very expensive), and especially avoiding oil-based glues. Many old labels have been ruined by brown stains from such glues that have seeped through from the back to the front. Mike Jones's recommended method is to use starch paste or another animal- or vegetable-based glue if you want to stick your labels permanently into an album, but use stamp hinges if you think you might need to take them off their backing occasionally. Acid-free paper is only for purists, but good-quality medium-weight paper, around 100gsm, should be used, and ring binders or lever-arch files enable individual sheets of labels to be inserted or taken out.

## BEER CAPS

Along with the zip fastener and the paperclip, the crown cork bottle top is one of those nineteenth-century inventions so ubiquitous that we barely notice it, or at least we don't bother to think about the intellectual efforts that went into its initial creation. Today, billions of tops a year are manufactured, capped onto bottles, and later flipped off by consumers who have never heard of William Painter, the American who patented the crown cork more than a century ago, in 1892.

Painter had already patented one form of beer bottle closure, the 'loop seal,' in 1885. It looked like a rubber bath plug without the chain, and it was one of more than a dozen competing bottle closures. But the crown cork quickly swept almost all rivals away. Its invention was the culmination of years of effort into designing a reliable bottle seal that could be applied quickly by machine and removed equally easily by the purchaser.

The traditional bottle cork was labor-intensive to apply, because it required wiring down to prevent it flying out under the pressure inside the bottle, and

it was difficult to remove. Many different solutions had been tried: in Britain the screwtop had been invented in the 1870s, and was in wide use by brewers by the mid-1890s, but it could not be adapted easily to mechanical bottle filling. In continental Europe and America the swing-top 'Lightning' porcelain stopper was widely used, but again it was labor-intensive to install, even though it had the advantage that the bottle could be resealed.

## HOW CROWN CORKS WORK

The crown cork – in actuality a seal rather than a stopper – was crimped tightly onto the top of the bottle, and stayed there until it was no longer required. It was cheap, its application was easily mechanized, and it enabled brewers to produce bottled beers much faster and more cheaply than with any other sort of closure. Until the invention of the screw-off crown cork in the 1960s it always required a special opener to get the top off, but customers did not seem to mind this inconvenience.

In 1893 the Crown Cork and Seal Company of Baltimore, Maryland, was declaring that its stoppers were 'the most perfect system of bottle stoppering ever invented,' being 'far superior to patent stoppers or corks, in tightness, keeping qualities, security, cleanliness, and purity of goods, ease of opening, and handsome, elegant appearance.' The crowns would stand up to an internal bottle pressure of 150 pounds per square inch, the company said, they were cheap to fit, 'although there is no suggestion of "cheapness" in its appearance,' and they did not need to be wired down while the bottles were being pasteurized.

The design has changed a little over the years. Original crown corks literally contained a circle of cork inside to keep the beer away from the metal of the top. Natural cork was replaced by 'composition cork' around 1907, which turned out to have two advantages: it was cheaper, and it leaked less. By the 1960s cork was replaced with a plastic liner. Crowns can let oxygen into the bottle around their edges, which will speed up the processes that make beer go stale, and today some brewers incorporate an 'oxygen scavenger' melded into the crown. The twist-off top is widespread in America and the Far East. However, William Painter would find his original idea effectively unchanged in 110 years.

# Labels & tops

Despite its advantages, it took some time for the crown cork to be accepted, partly because it meant an investment in new machinery. The authoritative history of William Painter's invention, *Crowns, The Complete Story*, written by John J Nurnberg and published in the 1950s, pointed out that:

> 'When crowns first came into use, the bottles were all handmade and the lip diameters and lip shapes varied considerably. Such variations could be accommodated in the early crowners, which were foot operated. However, with the introduction of high-speed automatic crowners, more uniform bottles became necessary. The glass industry had to adopt a standard bottle for the standard crown.'

Pre-Prohibition advertising in America confirms that crowns were quickly adopted by brewers such as Miller of Milwaukee, Wisconsin, which used them for High Life; by Anheuser-Busch; by Pabst; and by Voigt of Detroit, Michigan, for its Rheingold; and many others. (Ordinary corks were still in wide use simultaneously, however.) Several brewers had noticed that trademarks and slogans could be lithographed onto the tops of crowns. Elsewhere around the world, companies were slower to accept crown corks. They seem to have been entirely absent in British beer advertising before World War I, and Australian brewers only started using them around 1914, the year Cooper's of Adelaide, in South Australia, purchased its first crown corking machine.

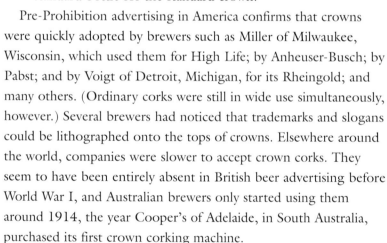

Soon after the end of Prohibition in America, the crown cork faced the challenge of canned beer. The Crown Cork Company fought back with the 'cone top' can sealed with a standard bottle top, but this eventually gave way to the greater convenience of the flat-top can. However, bottled beer is still hugely popular around the world, which means that the crown cork, despite its age, has life left in it yet.

There are large numbers of collectors of crown corks in America and continental Europe; the biggest collection is claimed to be that of Günter Offermann of Hamburg in Germany, who estimates he has more than 85,000 different crowns from 173 countries. Collecting crown corks is effectively unknown in Britain, though. The obvious attraction of crown collecting is the same appeal of any miniature work of art. Brewers have sometimes been able to

produce remarkable designs on these tiny throwaway pieces of metal. There is at least one magazine, *Crowncappers' Exchange*, produced in America, and another, *Cap Collector*, published in Europe. Crown cap collectors also have some of the best websites on the World Wide Web.

Crowns are an easy item to collect on trips abroad or at home. Like bottles themselves, unusual crowns from obscure places and breweries are becoming easier to find as package stores and supermarkets increase their ranges of beers. Asking friends or relatives to bring back crowns from their trips away is another simple way of increasing your collection. Just give them a bottle opener before they set out, and make sure they are aware of how to open a bottle without damaging the cap.

## REMOVING CROWNS

Indeed, the biggest problem facing crown collectors *is* how to get the top off the bottle without damaging it. Of two identical-looking bottle openers, one might lift a top off without a scratch or dent, and the other might leave the cap irreparably bent. Some collectors recommend putting a coin or similar round, hard object between the crown and the opener, to avoid dents and damage. Others go for the 'over-the-top' opener, which grips a far larger proportion of the cap and avoids any risk of bending. Another type of bottle opener, American-made, is called the Perfect Opener Pal. Using it upside down and 'pushing down' rather than 'levering up' will give minimal damage to the crown as it leaves the bottle, its fans say.

Storage of crowns can be a problem. They are too bulky for binders or similar, and loose tops can scratch each other. Sticking crowns to anything permanently makes rearranging your collection impossible, and, remember, it ruins their collecting value. Some people have used the sticky-back magnetic strips sold in electronics stores to attach crowns to metal surfaces (they make nice refrigerator magnets). One good solution is probably the drawers used by coin or medal collectors. A less expensive but related idea is to find a coin collectors' shop selling black cardboard coin mounters with holes of the size that takes the standard crown cork. Another possibility is to have your local picture frame shop make up glass-fronted trays with dividers that enable each crown to be kept separate.

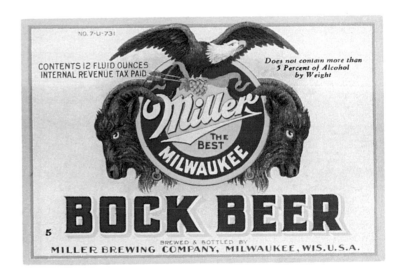

**Above** A late nineteenth-century Pabst label for one of the company's seven brands, Hofbräu, issued shortly after the brewery name was changed in 1889 from Phillip Best.

**Right** A nineteenth-century label bearing the name Adolphus Busch, rather than Anheuser-Busch, and printed in Leipzig, Germany. Perhaps no American printer could cope with the large quantities of labels Busch wanted when he first began bottling beer for large shipments, in 1873.

**Top and above** A couple of early pre-Prohibition labels from Miller, showing High Life described as 'Münchener' (or Munich) style, that is, dark brown rather than light, and bock beer with the obligatory goats (bock being the German for goat, as well as the name of a style of seasonal strong beer).

# Labels – United States

**Above** Since many Americans refer to beer as 'suds,' it was inevitable that one brewer somewhere would use Suds as a brand name. Spearman became part of the Metropolis Brewery Co.

**Above** Schlitz may be best known as a lager brand, but in the early years the brewery catered for wider tastes with its own porter.

**Above** It is doubtful that Tahoe Ale was really as 'Famous as the Lake,' since items from Carson Brewing of Nevada are generally described as 'rare.'

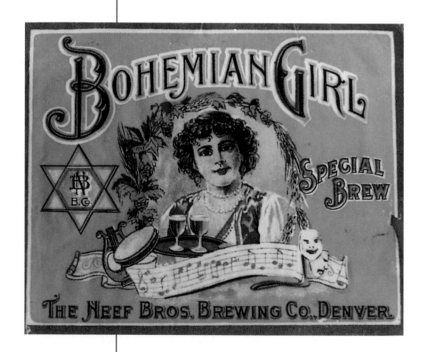

**Above** Coors' labels have changed very little over the years, as this mid-20th century example shows.

**Above** This label is a variation on the lithographer Louis Prang's image of 1890. The young Bohemian woman, her hair decorated with a hop wreath, originally advertised Stroh's Extra. Here she has been given a little red cap in addition to the hops.

**Left** A post-Prohibition label for an English-style IPA from Gottfried Krueger Brewing of Newark, New Jersey, with the Krueger 'K' man trademark making only a discreet appearance on the tankard held by the cheery drinker. The brewery's roots go back to the 1850s, but Gottfried Krueger only became a partner in 1865. Krueger finally closed in 1960.

**Above and left** A couple of labels from the Frankenmuth Brewing Co. in the town of the same name in Michigan, reflecting the mixed British-German heritage of so many American brewers. The brewery was severely damaged by a tornado in 1996.

## VARIATIONS ON THE BOCK BEER THEME FROM THE UNITED STATES

Bock is a style of strong, seasonal beer of German origin, and Bock is German for goat, hence the horned and whiskered heads that appear on all these labels.

# Labels – United States & Britain

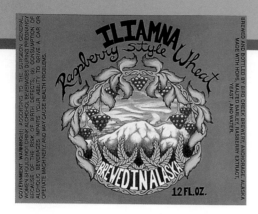

**THE PENNSYLVANIA BREWING COMPANY**

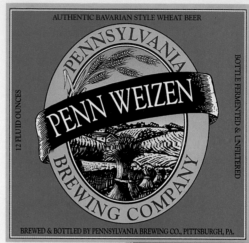

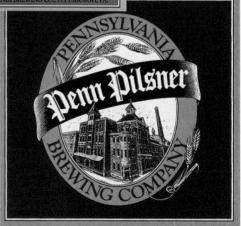

Five labels from American breweries of all ages: Anchor Steam of San Francisco, more than a hundred years ago; the Bird Creek brewery in Anchorage, Alaska, a modern microbrewer; Buffalo Brewing of Lackawanna, New York, another new micro; Yuengling, in Potsville, Pennsylvania, the oldest surviving brewery in the United States; and the Michigan Brewery.

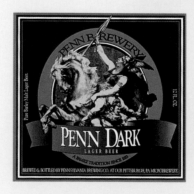

A set of labels from the Pennsylvania Brewing Company of Pittsburgh, another microbrewery founded in 1986, including one showing the old nineteenth-century Eberhardt & Ober brewery, where the new micro has made its home.

**Above** The 90/– on this label means 'ninety shillings,' originally the price per barrel of a strong beer, which gradually became the name of the beer itself. 'Shilling' designations for beers are still used by some Scottish brewers, though the shilling, one-twentieth of a pound, has not been in circulation since the British currency was decimalised 30 years ago.

**Above** Younger's Number 3 was once a famous and well-regarded Scotch ale, and this label, showing the Palace of Holyroodhouse in Edinburgh, would have been found in very many bars. The beer was last brewed in May 1998.

**Above** The beer is interesting – stout designed to perk up the sickly – but the bottler is even more interesting. John Roberts ran what was one of the last four surviving original home brew pubs in England in the early 1970s, at the Three Tuns, Bishop's Castle, Shropshire. The pub still brews today, an inspiration to the microbrewery revolution.

**Below** An unusual diamond-shaped label from a brewery in the northwest of England. It was taken over in 1966 and closed 1974.

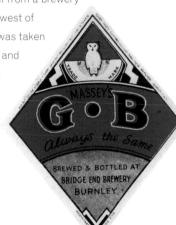

**Above** Rarer than it looks, this colorful label was issued in the 1890s, when the brewer, Fremlin's was a pioneer of bottled beers among English brewers.

**Above** The Burton on Trent brewer Ind Coope liked to lay exclusive claim to Double Diamond as a brand name for a beer, but the English South Coast brewer Brickwoods of Portsmouth went so far as to issue a double-diamond-shaped label.

**Right** Old is a type of mature strong beer, and mild is a younger, weaker ale, and they were often combined on draft by British drinkers ordering a half pint of each in the same glass. The Scottish brewer Blair's, which ran from 1853 to 1959, produced a bottled beer which did the same thing.

**Right** Considering the reputation of the 'fighting Irish,' Knuckleduster Stout might not have been the best brand name for this beer from the Cork brewer Beamish and Crawford in the 1950s.

# Labels – Britain

## DISTINCTIVE BRITISH LABELS OF THE 1950s

A set of six 1950s labels from around England, including a Russian Imperial Stout with the 'Dr Johnson' trademark of Barclay's of London; Case's, which closed in 1972; and the Barnsley Brewery, closed 1976, whose name has been revived by a Yorkshire microbrewer.

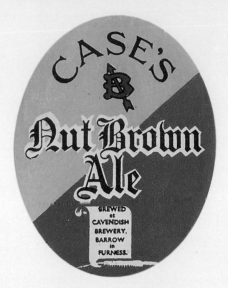

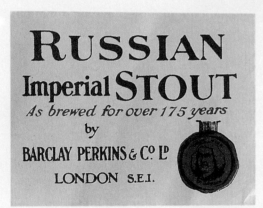

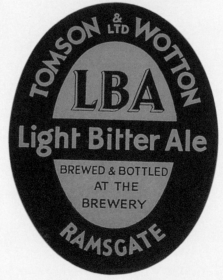

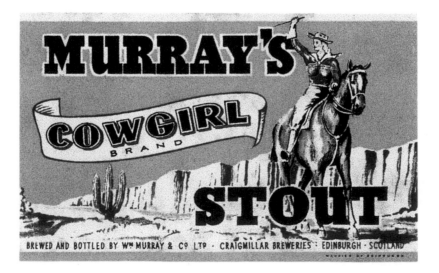

**Left** Not an American beer, but one from the Scottish brewer William Murray of Edinburgh – though who knows what the link was meant to be between cowgirls and stout. Murray's closed in 1963.

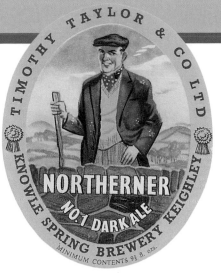

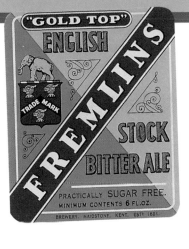

Eight British labels from the 1960s and early 1970s including an oddity from the Manchester brewer JW Lees for a container of just under four pints of lager; a label from the nationalized Carlisle State Brewery; Theakston's of Masham's Old Peculier spelt the more normal way as it is on older labels; and variations on the 'Huntsman' logo originally licensed to three different brewers in the 1930s.

# Labels – European

**Above** The label from a Munich-style beer made by the White Cross brewery in Santander, Spain around 1910. The brewery finally closed in 1985.

**Above** An elaborate label with a German name from the Estrella de Gijon brewery in Spain which looks as though it was made much earlier than its actual date of 1950.

**Above** Three Pilsen labels from the LA Salve brewery in Bilbao, Spain, all from around 1950.

A line-up of five labels from the White Rose brewery in Palma de Mallorca in the Balearic islands, all around 50 years old.

**Above** Two stylish 1920s labels from the Santa Barbara brewery in Madrid, Spain, which was sold to Union Cervecera in 1940.

# Labels – European

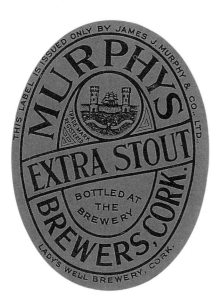

**Above** A 'hell' (pale) beer from the Grieskirchen brewery in Upper Austria.

**Above** A couple of 1950s labels from the two breweries in Cork, Ireland.

**Above** Ritterbrau (knight's brew) from the brewery at Neumarkt am Hausdruck in Austria.

**Above** Two old labels from Hamburg's Holsten brewery.

**Above** Two Polish examples from the Bojanowo brewery.

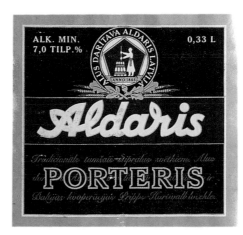

**Above** A label from a bottle of porter brewed by Aldaris in Riga, capital of the Baltic republic of Latvia.

**Above** The premium brand from Amstel of The Netherlands, whose beers are still brewed by Heineken, which took the company over in the 1960s.

**Above** One from early in the twentieth century and the village of Hobro on the Danish mainland.

**Above** One from Sweden's Falcon brewery for 'Bayerskt,' a dark Munich-style lager.

**Above** A label for Denmark's second best-known beer, Tuborg.

# Labels – International

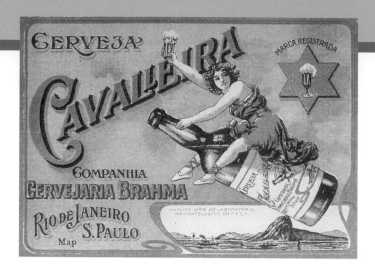

**Above** Early twentieth-century labels from Brahma, still one of Brazil's leading brewers (note the 'brewer's star' trademark) and the Blumenauense brewery, showing the German influence on the country's brewing trade.

**Above** One of the earliest known Canadian labels, from around 1860, issued by Molson of Montreal, Quebec.

**Above** Clara, the name of this beer from pre-independence Mozambique, means 'pale' in a beery context, though it may also be the name of the young lady on the label.

**Above** The goat the young lady is kissing on this mid-twentieth-century label from Luxembourg identifies the brew inside the bottle as a bock beer.

**Above** An early label from the Santa Fé brewery in Argentina, still running today in Buenos Aires.

**Above** The oil wells at Baku, source of the country's wealth, feature on this label from Azerbaijan.

**Above** It looks Danish at first glance, but close inspection shows this label, issued in 1998, is from the Nuuk Imeq brewery in Greenland.

**Above** This Indian label from the 1910s was printed in the United States.

**Above** A curious stein-shape label issued by the Egmondville brewery in Ontario, Canada, between 1904 and 1913.

**Above** A celebratory label from pre-World War I Venezuela, brewed for the 100th anniversary of the start of the revolution that eventually led to the country's liberation.

**Above** The name of the brewery on this 1890s label from Ecuador suggests it was set up by North Americans. Guayaquil still has a brewery today.

# Labels – International

## CHINA – A LAND RICH IN BREWERIES

Four labels from China, three from Tangshan, near Peking, and one from Guangyulan. There are an estimated 850 breweries in China, making it the third most 'breweried' country in the world after Germany and the United States.

**Above** The Himalayas, unsurprisingly, feature on this pre-World War II label from Nepal, which boasts of German assistance.

**Above** Nelson's Column in London graces this label from the Murree Brewery Company, which opened its branch brewery in Rawalpindi in modern-day Pakistan in 1889. The original brewery at Ghora Gali, founded in 1861, was closed in 1927, and production concentrated in Rawalpindi, which is still open today.

**Above** A beer label from communist North Korea which has taken the name of the country's capital, Pyongyang.

Beer brewing in Islamic countries has a dogged history of survival, despite alcohol being frowned upon. This set of labels is from Iran, where, **clockwise from right,** a bonneted Scotsman advertises something called 'Pilsene beer;' the Blue Nile Brewery, opened in Sudan in 1955 by the British brewery company Barclay Perkins and still brewing Camel lager today; Libya, with no concession at all to non-Arab speakers; and two 'Stellas' from Egypt and Jordan. **Top** The Eastern Brewery, Baghdad, Iraq; Taybeh, a comparatively recent brewery in Palestine;

# Labels – International

## A TRIO FROM SOUTHEAST ASIA

Three labels from Southeast Asia, one original South Vietnamese beer with the name and logo of the French-owned BGI, Brasseries et Glacières de l'Indochine; the next from Laos looking heavily influenced by BGI; and the last from Cambodia.

**Above** An astonishingly rare label from the Oriental Brewery of Hong Kong, which ran only from 1910 to 1912.

**Above** A pre-World War 2 label from a French-run brewery in Syria which combines very art-nouveau influenced lettering with Arabic decoration.

**Above** Before Castlemaine XXXX, there was Castlemaine XXX, a pre-1928 stout from the Brisbane, Australia, brewer with a curious logo of a lapdog.

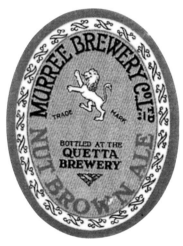

**Above** Another, older Murree Brewery label, this one from the Quetta branch brewery in India, which was destroyed by an earthquake in 1935.

**Right** Simpson & Hart of Weatherstones, New Zealand closed in 1923 after a comparatively brief existence.

**Above** This label from Mongolia seems to imply that the local habit is to drink beer from glass teacups.

**Above** A lovely old label, *circa* 1900, from the Burmese branch of an Indian brewer now known as Mohan Meakin, maker of Kingfisher lager, after a merger in 1935.

**Above** An unusually-shaped label from one of the more obscure breweries to have come out of the Philippines.

**Above** The German influence on Latin American brewing is clear from this label of bock beer from Paraguay.

**Above** Some of the most striking labels in the world are the ones used by the South Pacific Brewery of Port Moresby, Papua New Guinea, set up by gold prospecting Australians in the 1940s who were frustrated at the lack of decent local beer.

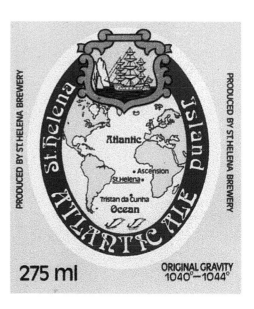

**Above** The short-lived St Helena brewery, based on the tiny South Atlantic island of the same name, lived and died in the 1990s.

# Labels – International

## SOUTH AFRICAN BREWERIES – ALE WITH A DISTINCTIVE STYLE

Seven old labels from breweries in Southern and Eastern Africa, including Lion double stout from Salisbury, the city now known by its original name of Harare, capital of Zimbabwe, and a British-style strong ale from South African Breweries, better known today for its Castle lager.

Four labels from Latin America, showing the local tendency to put a pretty girl on the bottle, from the Dominican Republic, Peru, Venezuela and Uruguay.

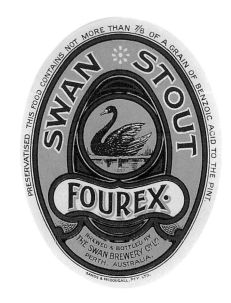

A diverse selection of Australian labels of different vintages from Perth in the west to Ballarat in the east, showing that 'Fourex' need not mean a pale-colored beer from Brisbane.

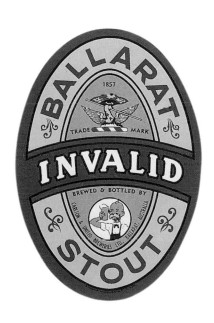

# Labels – Celebratory & Christmas

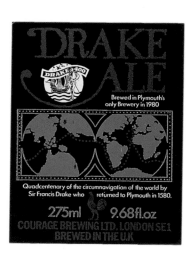

Celebratory labels from Britain for the British Horological Association; the Home brewery, Nottingham's centenary; the coronation of George VI in 1937; the coronation of his daughter Elizabeth II in 1953; her silver jubilee in 1977; the 400th anniversary of Sir Francis Drake's circumnavigation of the globe in 1980; the marriage of the Prince and Princess of Wales in 1981; and a visit by King Edward VII to the Bass brewery in 1902.

Christmas labels from Denmark (hvidtol is actually a type of weak table beer, knocking on the head the idea that all Christmas beers are strong); Cobb's of Kent, England (closed 1971); Herforder, in north Germany; Guinness; the island of Fano, Denmark; the Heritage brewery, Burton upon Trent, England, formerly Everard's; and Norway.

# Tops

**Right** An example of what can be collected from a single brewer. A selection of several dozen different crown corks, all from Stroh, some from the company's subsidiary breweries.

**Left** A case of North American bottle tops from Montreal's McAuslan; the Catamount brewery in Vermont; HC Berger of Fort Bragg, Colorado; the Boston Brewing Company's Samuel Adams Dark Wheat; Frederick Brewing of Maryland's Hempen Gold; Golden Pacific of Berkeley; California; Pike Place Brewery (now Pike Brewing) in Seattle; Henry Weinhard's, once owned by Stroh, now part of the giant Miller concern; Allagash of Portland, Maine; the distinctive top from a bottle of Anchor beer, San Francisco; BridgePort Brewing of Portland, Oregon; Schlitz, a once-renowned brewing name now in the hands of Pabst; Old Dominion of Virginia; and cherry beer from Pete's of California.

**Right** A short European tour of crown corks includes an anniversary top from Poland's Okocim brewery (pronounced 'Okkocheem'); Carlsberg of Denmark's Christmas top; Munich's Hofbrau; the Gouden Boom (Golden Tree) brewery in Bruges, Belgium; the small Thisted brewery in Denmark; the Castelain brewery in northern France, whose Ch'ti beers bear a coalminer logo; Oranjeboom of The Netherlands; Spain's Aguila; Maisel, from Bayruth, Germany; Falkensteiner, also from Germany; Prague's Vratislavice brewery; a Tripel top from the Westmalle Trappist brewery in Belgium; and a dark beer from a north German brewer, Beck's, best known for a pale lager.

# Tops

**Right** British brewers have not been left behind in the challenge to make collectable crown corks. This double-handful includes Gordon's, a strong ale made in Edinburgh for the Belgian market; St Andrew's Ale, from the Caledonian brewery, also in Edinburgh; a top from King & Barnes of Sussex; one of the 'Vintage Ale' tops from Ushers of Trowbridge, Wiltshire; Fuller Smith & Turner of London's '1845', the year the partnership was founded; Strong Suffolk from the Greene King brewery; the bulldog on the top of the Nethergate Brewery of Suffolk's Old Growler; the purple top from Young's of London's Double Chocolate Stout; the 'standard' top issued by Fuller's; a special top for Scottish Courage's Blue Star bottled ale; the armorial bearings used by Marston's of Burton-upon-Trent; the Welsh dragon of Brain's of Cardiff; and the Lincolnshire brewer Bateman's windmill logo.

**Left** The worldwide collecting possibilities of crown corks are captured in this selection from New Zealand, Jamaica, Japan, Florida, the Philippines, India, Australia, Singapore, Thailand, Siberia, South Africa, Trinidad, and China.

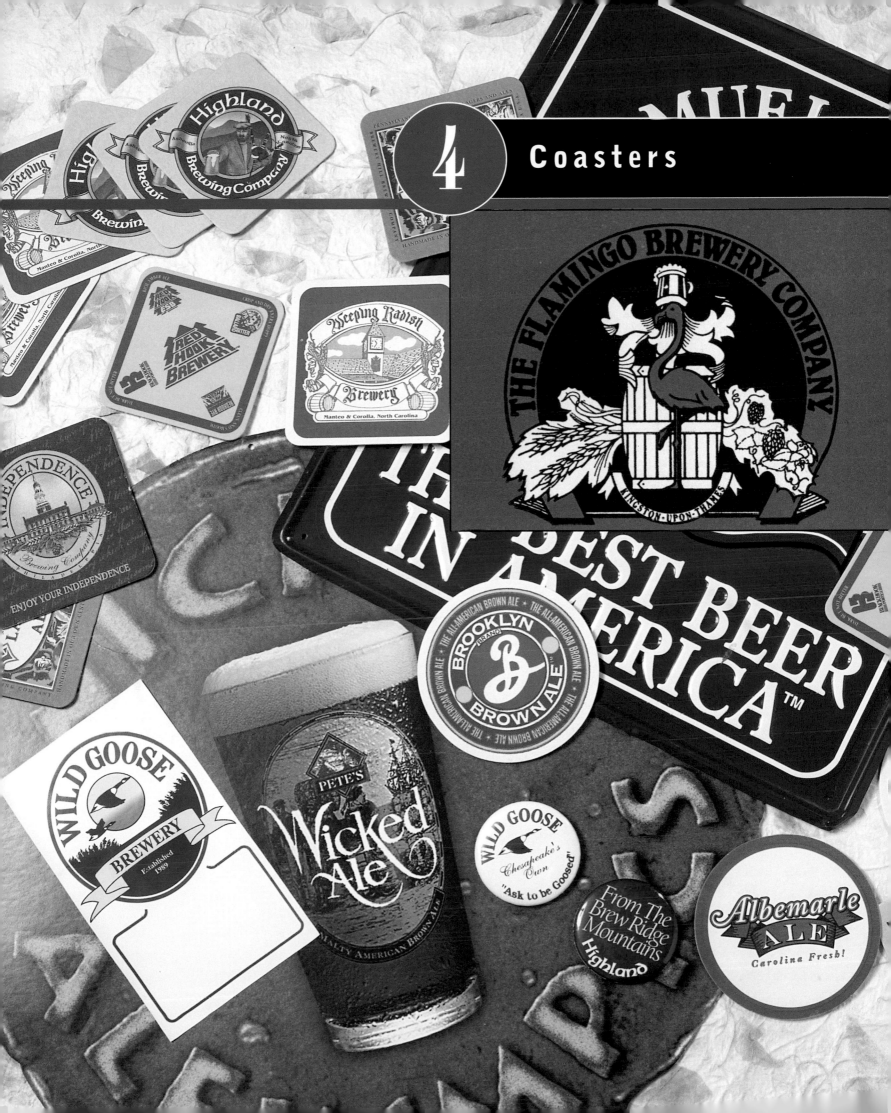

# Coasters

**F**ew throwaway items are more collected than the wood-pulp dripmat. The disposable cardboard mat, capable of carrying printed advertising, was patented in Dresden, Germany, in 1892 by Robert Sputh. (However the French insist that the first patent for an 'undercup sponge' was registered in June 1892 in Paris.) It was a cheap and cheerfully colored replacement for the lipped china or metal 'coaster' used to protect polished tables from wet-bottomed decanters or bottles. Some china coasters issued by breweries in the nineteenth century have survived, but they have been overwhelmingly outnumbered by their cardboard cousins.

'Coaster' is the normal word for the modest wood-pulp dripmat in the United States, Australia, and New Zealand, but the British insist on calling them beermats. From beermat the fanciful name for coaster collecting is derived: 'tegestology,' after the Latin *teges*, meaning little mat. In German a dripmat is commonly called a *Bierdeckel* or, occasionally, a *Bierfilz* (literally 'beer-felt,' as in felt blanket or mat), while Dutch has the related word *bierviltje*. In France they are *sous-bocks* and in Italy *sottobicchieri*, both meaning literally things that go under glasses.

The dripmat made its way to the United States around the beginning of the twentieth century, often being printed in Germany for American brewers. It did not appear to reach Britain until the 1920s, and other European countries were even later in accepting coasters. Spain's first beermat, for example, from the El Aguila brewery in Madrid, was issued only around 1930.

The earliest-known British mats, from the London brewer Watney Combe Reid, are simple reproductions of oval bottle labels for Watney's pale ale and Reid's special stout, printed on larger circular dripmats, thus leaving a crescent of unused space either side of the design. Both mats have been dated to 1925, though putting a year to early dripmats is a notoriously imprecise art. Several mats confidently labeled 'pre-war' (meaning pre-1939) by proud collectors have had to be dated again when it was shown that the beer they advertised was not produced until much later.

One mat for Double Top bottled strong ale issued by the tiny Simpson's brewery in the town of Baldock, Hertfordshire, was claimed to be from 1934. However, although the mat is certainly old, it cannot be dated earlier than 1951, since that was the first year Simpson's brewed the beer. Printers' names are often a good guide to a mat's age. For example, one early British mat printer, Abbot Brown of Twickenham, Middlesex, went out of business around 1936, so any mats with that name below the design in small letters is bound to be mid-1930s or older.

## EARLY COASTERS

These early mats generally show a pocked surface, and they appear remarkably thick compared to modern mats: over the years mats became thinner and thinner, and smooth-surface mats began appearing around 1960. Early German and American mats are very well printed compared to British mats of the same era, which are often black-and-white only line-drawings. Many early British mats look like one printer's standard issue with the brewer's name overprinted to order, particularly those mats showing line-drawings of old pubs and inns, issued by several different brewers.

In the United States mats survived the restrictions of World War II, making wartime mats a popular collecting category. In Britain only one brewer, Offilers of Derby, is known to have issued a wartime mat. However, in both the US and Canada, various state and provincial authorities from California to Virginia have, at different times, banned brewers from distributing any advertising materials that could have a secondary value. This may be why coaster collecting is not as popular in America as, say, can collecting.

In Europe the story is completely different. Advertising coasters have been banned only in Sweden, as part of a general interdictment on drinks advertisements. The British Beer Mat Collectors' Society, founded in 1960, is the biggest beer memorabilia society in the country. Germany and Belgium have well-established collectors' organizations, and in Eastern Europe countries such as the Ukraine also have large numbers of mat collectors with their own clubs, holding regular meetings.

## EUROPEAN COASTERS

British and German collectors have spent years collating every known mat in sequence, and giving each mat from every national brewery its own unique number. Some breweries, such as Guinness, are now up into four figures of numbers of mats issued. One constant source of argument among collectors is what exactly constitutes a different mat. Different print-runs can result in noticeable differences in ink color, while the same mat can be stamped out with different cutters, giving, say, sharply rounded or more curved corners to a square mat. Should that be counted as a different mat or not? In the United States a coaster issued for Rheingold started off with the legend 'Brewers for over 115 years' on the bottom, with the figure rising for the next six years when the mat was reissued, ending with 'Brewers for over 121 years.' Completists would insist on having all seven coasters: many collectors would be happy with one.

The most notorious 'variorum' mat was issued by the English brewer Moorfield of Wigan, Lancashire, which in effect let its printer decide which two of 34 different colors to print the mats. Over the 14 years from 1957 to 1970 inclusive that the mat was in use, at least 112 color combinations were used for the words and the colored band across the middle of the mat. Collectors can only be thankful that this is still well short of the total possible number of combinations, 2,244! There are other variations in the mat's design, with different-size stars in the top left corner, and different-shape apostrophes in 'Moorfield's,' but most people overlook these discrepancies.

The collectability of coasters was recognized by brewers around 50 years ago, when they began issuing sets of mats. The London brewer Charrington printed a set of six mats in 1945 showing different sports, including cricket and swimming. One of the earliest sets was from the small English brewery McMullen's of Hertford, which printed a set of mats in 1957 showing old cars, that actually promised on the bottom: 'Collectors' first series of 12.' Subsequent series covered all kinds of transport, from boats through buses. Series of mats often try to inform: one set from Gettelman in Milwaukee, Wisconsin, before it was bought by Miller taught beer drinkers how to say 'cheers' in languages from Polish through Portuguese. The Bennett brewery in Newfoundland had a series of six mats showing incidents from Newfoundland's past. Spain's first set of mats, from the Union Cervecera group of breweries, did not arrive until as late as 1980. It showed street signs from 12 European capitals, and advertised Skol, a British lager brewed under license in Spain.

Sometimes mats need to be made into a set before you can read the message. The British brewery Worthington issued a set of six which each contained a segment of the brewery name, while in Ireland the Porterhouse microbrewery of Dublin had a series of mats each advertising a different one of its beers on one side, and each showing a different part of a bar scene on the other, which built up into the whole picture when you had the complete set.

## THE FIRST SHAPED MATS

The earliest mats and coasters were round, or square with rounded corners, or, occasionally, hexagonal. One of the first shaped mats was from Mitchell and Butler of Birmingham, England, which was cut to look like two glasses side by side. Probably the most irregularly shaped mat was the one issued by the Ann Street brewery of St Helier on Jersey, one of the Channel Isles, which was cut into the shape of the island. Another island-shaped mat was issued by the Albani brewery of Denmark, which was in the form of the Danish island of Fyn. Other shapes have included light bulbs, barrels, cans, and, from the Iroquois brewery of Buffalo, New York, a native American's head with war-bonnet.

Coasters celebrating particular events are rarer than commemorative bottled beers, but quite a few brewers issue special mats to commemorate their own

Left **A coaster for cans of Watney's Party Seven and Party Four, seven-pint and four-pint containers of what may well have been the worst beer in the world.**

# Coasters

Left **A stylish modern coaster from a small brewery in Pärnu, on the coast of Estonia.**

anniversaries, especially 'sesquicentenaries' (150 years) and bicentenaries. There are also mats marking such occasions as the 1948 Olympic Games in London, Queen Elizabeth II's silver jubilee, and the 1981 Royal wedding.

Coasters have been issued in other materials than card. Breweries have issued mats bearing their names in rubber, cork, plastic, linoleum, felt-covered foam, and something called pliadek (which is rubberized cheesecloth coated with flock). Whether these count as beermats is an arguable point, though they are certainly beer memorabilia. Sometimes brewers issue coasters that are definitely for home use rather than for the bar or pub. In the United States the West End Brewing Company of Utica, New York, was printing coasters on the side of its six-pack containers in the early 1960s that were perforated around the edges so that they could be torn out like postage stamps and used at home, while Murphy's of Cork, in Ireland, gave away leather-covered gold-embossed cork coasters in the 1980s.

## 'DRIP CATCHERS,' OR FLIMSIES

A sub-division or relative (depending on how you look at it) of coaster collecting is the 'drip catcher' or flimsy. These are made of tissue paper, and come in two types: either with a hole in the middle and a slit so that they can fit over the foot of the glass like a collar, or whole, like miniature round beermats with a deckle edge. They are popular in countries such as Germany and Austria where premium beer is regularly served in smaller glasses, but virtually unknown in places such as the British Isles.

Coasters are also, of course, issued by organizations other than brewers. Manufacturers of cigarettes, spirits, hard cider, and even pies and cheese have all distributed beermats, while coasters have also advertised airlines, books, jazz records, newspapers, television stations and car companies, and even police forces. They have been used to publicize road safety campaigns, county fairs, and, of course, beer festivals and individual bars and pubs. Sometimes television companies have had mats made promoting the fictional breweries featured in their 'soap operas.'

Coaster collecting is a worldwide hobby: even Iraq's Eastern Brewery in Baghdad has issued a beermat, and it is possible to build a collection covering many of the more than 120 countries that have breweries. If friends or family are traveling abroad, getting them to bring home a few coasters in their pockets is a lot kinder than asking for bottles and cans.

Indeed, acquiring new coasters is one of the easiest areas of beer memorabilia collecting. Your local bars are likely to have a constant supply. Of course, in many places you have to be over 18, 19, or 21 to go into a bar, but once you are in, if you ask politely, most bar owners or managers will be happy for you to take one or two mats for your collection and for swaps. They will probably even let you have new, unstained copies from behind the bar, rather than used ones from the counter or tables. Do not just sneak them off the table or bartop though. Always remember that mats are designed for a practical purpose – to soak up spilt drink – and the bartender is not going to be happy about wiping down a wet table because you have slipped all the coasters into your pocket. In any case, taking without asking is theft.

## COLLECTORS' SOCIETIES

Obtaining spare mats is important, because if you want to get coasters issued by brewers outside your local area, you either have to travel a lot, or you can go along to collectors' meetings and exchange mats with other like-minded people. You can find coasters for sale at flea markets and collectors' fairs, but if you have been collecting for a while you will normally recognize them as common examples. If you join a collectors' society, you will find most have a regular publication which lists new issues of mats, to help you keep track of what is going on. They will also carry small advertisements with offers from other collectors. However some societies, like the British Beermat Collectors, ban the buying and selling of mats at society meetings and through their publications, because they feel that it brings too much commercialism into an amateur hobby. But straight swapping is permissible, and postal swapping is a good way to get coasters from far away. All societies have auctions of coasters, which is often the only way to acquire the very oldest ones. If you want to possess a pre-World War II coaster, however, save up your pennies – the three-figure mat was first seen at an auction nearly 20 years ago! Old coasters make up a specialist area available – unless you are lucky enough to be left a stash of ancient mats by an elderly relative – only to the wealthier collector. Most collectors specialize in the mats of their own country, and some in the mats of their region; others just try to collect as many coasters from as many different breweries and countries as possible. It is surprisingly easy to build a collection of a thousand coasters. All the same, this is still an area where you can acquire a rarity for nothing, thanks to the microbrewery boom. New small brewers in the United States and Britain do issue coasters, but often only in small numbers. One much sought-after mat from the Victoria brewery in Ware, England, founded in 1980, was issued for just one beer festival.

## HOW TO DISPLAY YOUR COASTERS

The way you display your coasters is very important if you want your collection to last. They are made out of cheap material which oxidizes very quickly, so that almost all older mats are turning brown. Old mats also fray at the edges, and should therefore be handled as seldom as possible. Small plastic bags used as covers for individual mats are a good idea for valuable old mats. Pinning your coasters to the wall, or sticking them up with tape or glue is a disaster; no collector will be interested in the mat after the damage you have inflicted on it. Leaving coasters out in the light for a long time is, in any case, a bad idea. Inks will fade and the surface will turn brown. Other problems are caused by storing coasters in lofts, where damp and heat can warp them, and they will also be open to attack both by mold and – believe it or not – woodworm! Their larvae will eat old wood-pulp coasters happily.

The bulk and weight of coasters mean displaying them in albums is impractical. Storing your collection in shoe-boxes or similar-size boxes, cardboard or plastic, is the best solution in many ways for the collector who is just starting out. The boxes are light and can be kept in cupboards, and card index dividers can be used to mark off different sections. Another cheap solution is to use the cardboard boxes in which

Left **Trinidad's best-known beer brand features on a bottle-top-shape coaster issued on the island itself.**

fruit is supplied to supermarkets. Again, card index dividers can be used.

Some collectors invest in the sort of wall-mounted hinged multiple-display frames found in museums, which you can close up to protect your collection from the light, and open out to show off your coasters to admirers. Such displays will hold around 600 coasters at a time. But they are expensive, they take up a lot of room on your walls you may not be able to spare, and they mean big disruption whenever you need to add a new mat to the display. For anyone whose collection is rising up toward the five figure mark, a dedicated chest of drawers is one answer. For example a drawer six inches tall, 30 inches wide, and 20 inches deep will comfortably hold more than 1,500 standard-size coasters, thus a four-drawer chest with drawers of these dimensions will easily accommodate a collection of 6,000 beermats.

## FLIP YOUR COASTERS

Finally, if you find yourself in a bar where the only coasters are ones you already have in your collection, there is still fun to have. Beermat flipping is a game of skill and dexterity, and one you can play on your own or with friends. Take a normal coaster, balance it on the edge of the table or bar so that not quite half the mat hangs out into space, and put your hand, palm down, about three inches below the mat. Lift your hand, striking the overhanging part of the coaster with the back of your fingers, and, as it spins in the air, catch it between your fingers and thumb. Now try it with two mats, then three, then four… Try it with a coaster for each hand simultaneously. Flip against friends, either increasing the number of mats each time until someone fails to catch cleanly, whereupon they are out of the game, or simply continuing to flip the same mat until someone fumbles. One word of warning, however: do desist if the bar staff ask you.

**Above** This coaster was part of a campaign by Anheuser-Busch for its Budweiser brand.

**Above** A coaster from the Muessel Brewing Co. of South Bend, Indiana. Like many early American coasters, it was printed in Germany.

**Above** Buckeye Brewing of Toledo, Ohio, lasted until 1966. Note the name of the coaster manufacturer: the Absorbo Beer Pad.

**Above** A pair of coasters from the now-closed Narragansett brewery of Cranston, Rhode Island, show that some brewers like to be famous for being famous – the brewery was using 'Famous' in its advertising way back in 1909.

**Above** A coaster from Watney's of London, England, which was proud of pioneering keg beer, later rented by the Campaign for Real Ales.

**Above** An old beer mat from Marston's of Burton on Trent, England, one of the great British brewing towns.

**Above** Fox Head 400 was the best-known brand in later years from Fox Head Brewing in Waukesha, Wisconsin.

**Above** Lees, one of Manchester, England's, long-lasting independent brewers.

**Above** The Ebling Brewing Co. was founded in the Bronx in 1840, and came through the Prohibition era to survive until 1951.

**Above** McEwan's of Edinburgh, now part of the Scottish and Newcastle brewery in Great Britain.

# Coasters – International

**Above** A pentagonal mat from Strong's of Romsey, Hampshire, England.

**Above** Iroquois Beverage Corporation of Buffalo, New York had one of the most striking trademarks of any American brewer.

**Above** Fremlins from the English hop country of Kent.

**Above** No messing: the Burtonwood brewery in northwest England issued this coaster showing its 'Top Hat' trademark and a claim to supreme superiority in the 1960s.

**Below** A punning coaster from Fuller Smith and Turner, when long-playing records, or LPs, were a novelty.

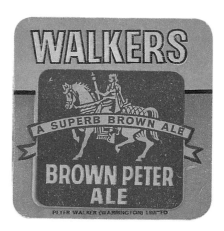

**Above** Peter Walker was the founder of Walker's brewery in Warrington, Cheshire, which grew to be one of the biggest in the North West of England.

**Above** United Clubs of Pontyclun, South Wales, was one of several breweries set up specifically to serve the workingmen's clubs trade with reasonably-priced beer. The brewery closed in 1989.

**Above** By 1974 the Blue Anchor in Helston, Cornwall, was one of only four surviving homebrew pubs in Britain. It has since been joined by hundreds more.

## WORLD WAR II COASTERS FROM POLAND

Four old coasters from Poland, all World War II or earlier: one for porter, a popular drink in the Baltic region from the Zywcu brewery, one from the Hugo Scobel brauerei in Gleiwitz (modern Gliwice) which stopped production after 1945, one from the E. Hasse brauerei, Breslau (modern Wroclaw), which also stopped production after 1945, and one from the Beskiden brauerei in Saybusch (modern Zywiec) dated around 1940-44.

# Coasters – International

## OLD GERMAN COASTERS

Three old coasters from some of Germany's very many breweries.

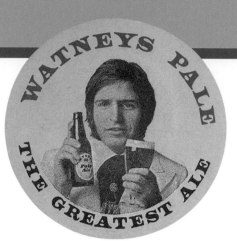

**Below** A coaster issued by the Yorkshire brewery Tetley's to celebrate the British Beermat Collectors Society's gold beermat award.

**Above** A 1960s British coaster with Beatle Paul McCartney's brother Mike for Watney's Pale Ale, reflecting a contemporary television ad that used the tune of Lily the Pink, a hit by Mike's band the Scaffold, to advertise the beer.

**Below** The lobster trademark and the brewery name are all that appear on this uncluttered and attractive coaster from DL Geary Brewing, a microbrewery from Maine.

**Above** The Pennsylvania Brewing Company, a microbrewery started in 1986, shows the old Eborhardt and Obor brewery on its coasters.

**Above** Simple and so very 1930s, a coaster from Alsace, Eastern France.

## US COAST TO COAST
## MICRO AND PUB BREWERS

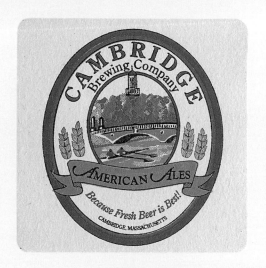

Five American micro and pub brewers crossing the country from coast to coast: West Side Brewing of New York, Cambridge Brewing from Massachusetts; Frederick Brewing of Maryland, whose Hempen Gold has been served on Air Force One, the Presidential aircraft; San Francisco Brewing Company; and Shipyard of Portland, Maine.

# Coasters – International

**Above** A coaster from the Saverne brewery in Alsace, France, with a warning used by brewers around the world – 'Never drink water, you don't know what's in it …'

**Above** An early 1920s coaster from France's Fischer brewery, also known by the French translation of its name, Pêcheur.

**Above** A coaster from Bosnia's capital Sarajevo boasts the brewery's age, and the medals it has won.

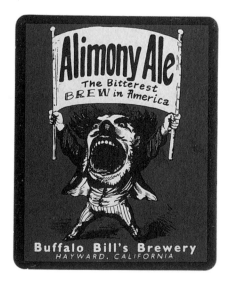

**Above** A coaster from Buffalo Bill's Brewery of Hayward, California. Alimony Ale was brewed after the acrimonious divorce of a colleague of the brewer.

**Above** The original Carling brewery operated in London, Ontario, between 1840 and 1936.

**Above** The eagle on this 1930s coaster from Spain's Aguila ('eagle') breweries carries the arms of the three cities where the company operated.

**Above** Boston Beer Company whose Samuel Adams lager is now an international brand.

**Above** The moustachioed beer drinker on this 1930s coaster from France bears comparison with the famous Moretti brewery's moustachioed man from Italy.

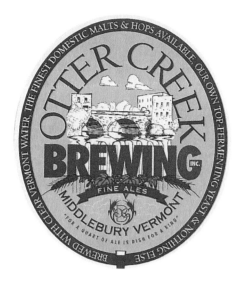

**Above** The Vermont based Otter Creek brewery, one of America's 'new' breweries.

**Above** Indonesia's best-known beer is Bintang. This coaster dates from the 1980s.

**Above** A coaster from Armenia that, unusually, includes the brewery's fax number.

**Above** A coaster from a West Coast contract brewer, Oregon.

# Coasters – International

**Above** The Boon Rawd brewery in Bangkok, Thailand, produces several beers, including the one featured on this coaster, Gold.

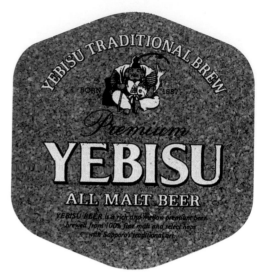

**Above** An unusual cork coaster from the Japanese brewer Sapporo.

THE 12-13TH CENTURY TEMPLE AT BELUR AND HALEBID ARE KNOWN FOR THIER INTRICATE CRAFTSMANSHIP. THE CHENNAKESHAVA TEMPLE ALONE HAS 42 BRACKET FIBURES OF WHICH THIS IS ONE. ONLY 222 KMS AWAY FROM BANGALORE, THE HOME OF **NIR .NA BEER**

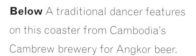

**Below** A traditional dancer features on this coaster from Cambodia's Cambrew brewery for Angkor beer.

**Above** Two sides of a coaster from Mysore Breweries of India for its Nirvana export beer, one side simply being a reproduction of the bottle label.

**Above** Nile Breweries of Uganda opened in the town of Jinja in 1954. Its ESB brand, on the right, is formally known as 'Chairman's Extra Strong Beer.'

**Above** A rare coaster from the Taybeh brewery, which started in the 1990s, and which proudly gives its address as Ramallah, Palestine.

**Above** This coaster from St Petersburg in Russia features a famous Russian hero.

## UNUSUAL COASTERS FROM GREAT BRITAIN

**Right** After David Bruce – who founded England's Firkin brewpub chain – sold up he started another chain, Hedgehog and Hogshead, but left soon after. This beermat dates from the early 1990s.

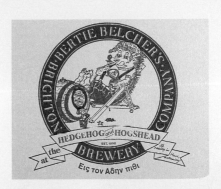

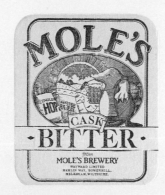

**Above** Mole's of Wiltshire has become one of Britain's most successful new breweries since it started in 1982. It now produces 10,000 (UK) barrels (14,000 US barrels) a year, and exports to the United States. This coaster was one of its earliest.

**Above** The Pitfield brewery in Hoxton, on the edge of the City of London, is now in its third home. This coaster dates from the late 1980s.

**Above** Another pink coaster, from Scotland's Alice brewery, Inverness, which ran from 1983 to 1987.

**Below** Pink is an unusual color in a bar, but appropriate, perhaps, for a brewery named for a flamingo. The brewery, in Kingston upon Thames, Surrey, England, was originally part of the Firkin chain, but ran under different ownership from the early 1990s until it closed in 1998.

**Above** A hop back is the vessel underneath the copper in a traditional brewery in which the hops collect when the boiled wort (raw beer) is run out, and the brewery's name is also a pun on the idea that its beers 'hop back' to the days of superior ales. Hop Back is based in Salisbury, England.

# Coasters – International

**FIRKIN FECUNDITY**

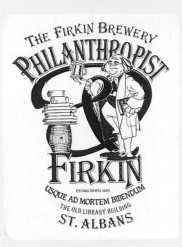

A selection of the many mats issued by the Firkin chain, which was founded in 1979 in London, England, and has now spread to France and The Netherlands. All the first Firkin pubs brewed their own beer: now only a quarter of the nearly 200-strong chain brew. Of those shown here, only the Philanthropist and the Fox have breweries attached. The Philanthropist is named for Andrew Carnegie, the American steel magnate, being based in a former library in St Albans, England, founded by Carnegie's charitable donations.

**Right** The Traquair House brewery in the Borders region of Scotland, based in an ancient stately home, was opened again in 1965 by the 20th Laird of Traquair, Peter Maxwell Stuart, after a gap of 150 years.

**Left** Another short-lived English brewery, Swannell's of King's Langley, Hertfordshire, which ran from November 1982 for a year. A former assistant brewer at Swannell's, Oliver Hughes, later helped found the Porterhouse Brewery in Dublin.

**Above and left** Two coasters from the short-lived English Home Counties boutique brewery Mickles of the early 1980s. It was founded by Mick Burch and Les Kent, hence the name of the brewery and its beers.

**Above** Six British coasters issued for special occasions: an FA World Cup mat from Watney's issued for the soccer championships of 1966, held in England; a Welsh mat issued, in Welsh, 10 years later for that year's Eisteddfod, or Bardic festival (Bro Buckley means land of Buckley, that being the name of the brewer); a rare mat from the 1948 Olympic Games in London, issued by the local brewer Taylor Walker; an anniversary mat for MG sports cars of Abingdon, issued by Morland, the town's brewer; and two mats issued for the 25th anniversary of Queen Elizabeth II in 1977 by the London brewer Courage and the Midlands' brewer Bank's.

**Right** Coaster from one of Japan's biggest brewers, Asahi, issued especially for Expo '70.

# Coasters - odd-shaped

**Above** Burts, the brewer from the Isle of Wight, off the south coast of England, used an outline of the island on its coasters, while **below**, the Scottish brewer Belhaven issued several versions of its 'Belhaven Bill' coaster.

**Top** A coaster from the Liverpool, England brewer Higson's in the shape of a 'polypin,' or 36-pint plastic beer container in a cardboard box, meant to give the beer fan draft ale at home. **Above** A mat from the Manchester, England brewer Wilson's showing its checkerboard trademark. **Below**, a 1960s mat from the English brewer Flowers for its Brewmaster pale ale. The brewmaster wears the red stocking cap and apron of his trade.

**Top and above** Yorkshire, England's, Black Sheep microbrewery has the sheep butting out of the side of the coaster, while this 1960s mat from Flower's, again, is in the shape of its pioneering aluminum keg. **Below**, a coaster from the East Anglian brewer Greene King for its short-lived Polar chilled ale from the early 1970s.

**Above** A crown cork-shaped coaster advertising Mann's, the best-selling brown ale in the UK.

# Ceramics & glass

Beer and pottery have been associated for thousands of years. Some archeologists believe that brewing could not have started until human beings learned to make pots to hold the fermenting wort. In the Middle East, where cultivation of wheat and barley began, there is a gap of thousands of years between the first evidence of settled agriculture and the first appearance of pottery, around 5500BC.

Pottery supplies the earliest evidence of beer brewing, through deposits found in jars used in Mesopotamia about 3600BC, and in pre-dynastic Egypt about 3200BC. Seals used to make markings on wet clay, left at sites in Sumer 5,000 to 6,000 years ago, show people drinking through straws out of tall, wide-mouthed, pointy-bottomed jars. It is believed that the straws were used because the beer was unfiltered and therefore contained grain husks floating on top. Egyptian brewers made 'bread-beer' by pressing wet bread through flat basket strainers into pottery jars, pouring water on it and letting wild yeasts ferment the bready liquid into beer. Clay models of brewers engaged in mashing up the bread have been found in Egyptian tombs, and the hieroglyph for 'beer' included a pictogram of a jar with a flat basket on top.

Pottery continued to be used in brewing for many thousands of years. Domestic brewers in medieval England used large pots having a capacity of around 19 gallons, with a bunghole placed just above the base so that the sediment would be undisturbed as the ale was drawn off. Whether these were just for storage, or for the actual brewing, is not clear. In the late nineteenth century beer for home use was often delivered in pottery half-gallon, gallon, or two-gallon stoneware containers, with a tap at the base and a screwtop. Stoneware was also used for making ginger beer bottles and, occasionally, for stout bottles.

Left **A lidded stein, from Sioux Falls Brewing and Malting Co. of South Dakota, which closed in 1919.**

## THE BEAKER FOLK

Pottery was generally replaced in brewing by wooden and metal vessels, once the technology to make watertight barrels and tubs had been acquired. But it continued, of course, to be used for drinking vessels. The Beaker Folk, whose burial sites are found all over northern and western Europe, dated at between 6,000 and 4,000 years ago, get their name from their pottery 'beakers' or drinking vessels, which were left in their graves. Later 'beakers' sometimes have strap handles and shapes which look just like pottery beer mugs, and the remains found inside show they were probably used for drinking some mead-based drinks.

Pottery has always had rivals among drinking vessels. Animal horns were popular with Celtic and Germanic drinkers, even after the arrival of Christianity. An Irish poem of the seventh century AD demands of challengers to the throne of Leinster:

> 'Are yours the drinking-horns of the wild ox?
> And is yours the ale of Cualu?'

Cualu (or Cuala) was the rich farmland area of east Leinster, where some of the best malting barley in Ireland was grown. Other drinking vessels were made of wood. The mazer was a maplewood bowl, turned and hollowed on a lathe, and bowls appear as beer drinking vessels in several medieval drawings: even in 1635 'beare bowls' are mentioned as part of a tavern's stock. Hooped wooden pots were also used. In Shakespeare's *Henry VI* the rebel Jack Cade declares that when he is king seven halfpenny loaves will only cost a penny and 'the three-hooped pot shall have ten hoops.'

Another common beer-drinking vessel was the black-jack, made of two pieces of leather sewn together, one for the sides and the other for the base, which was then sealed inside with pitch. It was replaced by mugs and tankards made of pewter, originally an alloy of tin and lead, which was introduced into England by the Dutch in the Middle Ages. Pewter tankards were apparently common in the American colonies in the seventeenth century and in Hogarth's eighteenth-century engraving of *Beer Street* everybody is drinking from quart pewter mugs (the traditional 'pot') except the impoverished pawnbroker, who can only afford a pint. Pewter beermugs were still found in the classier saloon bars of London in the 1950s, but they are limited to a few pretentious bars today. Silver tankards (a tankard, properly speaking, has a cover, and anything without a cover is a mug) were in use among the gentry until the nineteenth century.

Left **A cat-shaped stein from Germany bearing the Latin exhortation 'let us now be joyful.'**

### THE POPULAR STEIN

However, in German-speaking lands the stein, a pottery beermug made from clay mixed with flint or sand, has been the traditional beer-drinking vessel for centuries. The habit of drinking from steins was brought to America by nineteenth-century German immigrants, along with the habit of drinking lager. Steins have been made in many different shapes, and decorated with all sorts of pictures, quite a few carrying brewers' names. At the end of the nineteenth century the brewery stein or mug was a common giveaway from American brewers, and quite a few colorful examples with brewers' names and trademarks have survived to be appreciated by beer memorabilia lovers. Their attractiveness makes these early examples expensive for the ordinary collector.

It is a little-known fact that pottery beermugs were once common in Britain in the poorer sort of pub or bar. What is particularly surprising is that the commonest color for British pottery beermugs was pink, as mentioned by George Orwell, the author of *1984* and *Animal Farm*, in an article about his 'favorite' pub in the *London Evening Standard* in 1946.

'They are particular about their drinking vessels at the [mythical] Moon Under Water … apart from glass and pewter mugs, they have some of those pleasant strawberry-pink china ones which are now seldom seen in London. China mugs went out about thirty years ago [that is, around the time of World War I] because most people like their drink to be transparent, but in my opinion beer tastes better out of china.'

These straight-sided, handled pink pint beermugs, lacking the turned-over lip of the stein but recognizable because they have a crown and a royal cipher stamped into the glaze to show they hold the correct amount of liquid, turn up occasionally in junk and antique shops at very reasonable prices. Half-pint and quart versions are particularly rare, however. Other colors for British pottery beermugs are sky-blue and a rather more manly biscuit,

while pottery pint mugs are also known in the style called 'mocha,' with blue, and black bands on a white background and a tree-like design etched into the glaze.

Pottery has been used in the bar for more than just drinking vessels, of course. China ashtrays bearing brewers' names are very collectable. Pottery match strikers or matchbox holders were also issued by brewers for use in pubs. Brewery water jugs are numerous, and so are china figures illustrating brewery trademarks or slogans, from the Shakespeare's bust of Flowers of Stratford-upon-Avon, England, through the bust of the eponymous Shakespearian character issued by the Falstaff Brewing Corporation of America. Guinness has been responsible for a large number of pottery and ceramic collectibles, including models of the animals in the Guinness 'zoo,' lamp stands, and a set of three flying toucans, designed to be hung on a pub wall. These are a parody of the three flying china ducks that are found on the walls of many lower-middle-class British homes. Few microbrewers have released

Right **A Toby jug from the London brewer Hoare, of East Smithfield, London, England. Toby was Hoare's trademark, and when a rival London brewer, Charrington's, took over Hoare's in 1933 it readily adopted the Toby jug trademark as well.**

# Ceramics & glass

Left **A glass from the William Gerst Brewing Co. of Nashville, Tennessee, which brewed under that name from 1893 to 1919, and from 1933 to 1954. The '57' brand came out only in 1952.**

ceramic collectibles, though Pete Slosberg of Pete's Wicked appears as a beer-drinking baseball player in a seven-inch-high ceramic figure for 'Team Wicked.'

Although steins are popular among collectors, by far the commonest drinking vessel in bars and pubs is, of course, the beer glass. The beer-drinking Germans were making cone-shaped beakers of primitive *Waldglas*, or forest glass, in the fifth and sixth centuries AD. Most were tumblers, that is, they had no handle or base and could not be put down when full of beer. Some were even made in the shape of animal horns. One Saxon example of a glass drinking horn, found at Rainham in Essex, measured 13 inches from rim to tip.

Glasses do not seem to have been used much for ale or beer drinking before the seventeenth century, however. But about 1600 a taste grew in England among the gentry for very powerful pale hopped ales which were drunk out of comparatively small glasses holding just a quarter of a pint or less. These glasses were stemmed, with tall, straight sides. From around 1730 onward they were frequently decorated with engraved hop-and-barley motifs. In the late eighteenth and nineteenth centuries goblets, tumblers, and rummers (large-bowled, short-stemmed glasses) were also engraved with beery designs, and the half-pint glass rummer was frequently used for beer (and hard cider) in eighteenth-century English taverns. In Germany and Bohemia, meanwhile, glass mugs and tankards were appearing from the late sixteenth century.

The introduction of mold-pressed glass by the New England Glass Company of East Cambridge, Massachusetts, was a step on the way to mass-produced glass, which was encouraged in Britain by the repeal of the Glass Excise Act in 1845. At the same time pale ales and pale lagers were replacing dark beers and lagers in public taste around the world. Therefore brewers were seizing the opportunity to show off the sparkling quality of their products by serving them up in glass rather than stoneware, so that people could see the refreshing brew they were drinking.

Victorian beermugs are still thick and heavy, often fluted from the base to halfway up the sides. The plain, straight-sided,

handleless glass pint mug, remarkably similar to types still used in British bars today, appeared around the time of World War I. This type of glass was always vulnerable to damage to the rim, and by the 1960s a variant had appeared with a small bulge around the glass about an inch from the top. This is known as the 'Nonik' glass, because the bulge keeps the fragile rim from banging against the rims of other glasses, ensuring there will be 'no nicks.'

### FROM TEN-SIDED GLASSES TO 'DIMPLED STRAIGHTS'

By the end of the 1920s a type of glass ten-sided pint handled mug had arrived (half-pint versions have just nine sides) which many regard as the classic British ale glass: it is almost the only type of beer glass illustrated in the 'Beer Is Best' campaign paid for by the British Brewers' Society from the 1930s through 1950s, though British ale drinkers are divided 50/50 into those who prefer a handled mug and those who prefer a straight, handleless glass. In the 1950s the ten-sided glasses were replaced with 'dimpled' handled mugs. In the early 1980s there was a vogue for 'dimpled straights,' but these satisfied neither handle lovers not straight glass fans.

Few drink-specific beer glasses have evolved in Britain. A handleless 'jar' with a flattened 'S' shape to the sides is generally used for stout, perhaps because this is the commonest form of pint glass found in Ireland.

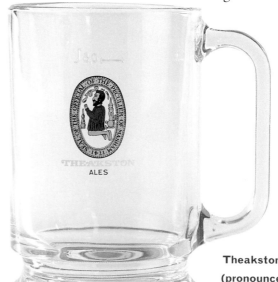

Guinness in the 1960s tried to promote the serving of its draft stout in graceful

Left **An unusual English footed pint glass from Theakston's of Masham (pronounced 'massam') in north Yorkshire, showing the seal of the peculier (sic) ecclesiastical court of Masham.**

Left **This tall, flared lager glass bears the 'Dr Johnson' trademark of Barclay Perkins of Southwark, London, England, which merged with its near-neighbor Courage & Co in 1955.**

handled tankards designed by Waterford Crystal, but these were unpopular with landlords and bar owners because they broke easily. The classic British bottled beer glass was a footed round-bottomed beaker, but this was used for everything from brown ale to barley wine. British drinkers would know to drink only lager out of a tulip-shaped glass (just such a glass, badged with the name of Carlsberg, featured at the end of the 1950s war movie *Ice Cold in Alex*), but they would also drink lager out of other sorts of glasses. Badged glasses are not common, but they are collected.

## A GLASS FOR EVERY DRINK

The home of the idea of a specific glass for every different type of beer is Belgium, where brewers often print pictures of the sort of glass you should or should not use for their beer on the back labels of their bottles. Strong abbey beers come in wide, flat-bowled glasses; pilsner lagers in tall, narrow glasses; golden ales in big, stemmed thistle-shaped glasses; and brown ales in straight-sided beakers. Almost all Belgian brewers produce a badged glass for each of their beers, and the glasses are highly collectable.

Germany also has a number of specific glasses for particular beers. These include the cylindrical glass used in Cologne to serve the city's specialty, Kolsch; the tall, narrow, waisted, heavy-bottomed glasses used for south German wheat beers; the big dimpled liter steins obligatory at events such as Munich's Oktoberfest. Again, many of the country's more than 1,000 brewers have brought out badged glasses.

In Australia, glasses vary from state to state, so that a 'schooner' in New South Wales will hold nearly twice as much as a South Australian 'schooner;' a 'glass' in Western Australia holds less than a 'glass' in Victoria, while Western Australia has three sizes of 'pot'

compared to Victoria's one. As in Britain, badged glasses are rare.

The microbrewery boom in the United States has meant an explosion of badged glasses for collectors, with getting on for 2,000 examples from brewpubs and small brewers now known. Most of these are bulgeless, straight-sided pint glasses. A few come in colored glass, and decoration varies from silk-screen printing through decals through sand-blasting and etching.

Glass has been used in bars for objects other than drinking glasses, of course. Brewers have produced mirrors and etched windows, and ashtrays also appear in glass. In the 1940s in America and the 1950s in Britain there was a fashion for glass ashtrays with bottle labels sealed into the base: unfortunately the sealing was not very effective, and the labels generally soon became damaged by water and/or abrasion.

Glasses and mugs can often be obtained via your friendly local bar (which will certainly not be happy if you take without asking, and they will prefer an offer to pay). Otherwise, like most other beery collectibles, they turn up at flea markets, garage sales, and collectors' fairs, and in junk shops, thrift shops, and the like. Pack them away carefully if you are unable to display everything you collect, and remember that a shelf loaded with ceramics puts a big strain on wall brackets. The occasional wash with warm soapy water, and careful drying, will keep your collection sparkling.

Left **The Belgian village of Silly has an eponymous brewery which produces a fine beer in the local** *saison* **style – but to English-speaking ears it sounds like 'silly season,' a term used by journalists for the quiet months of high summer, when any ridiculous story will get into the newspapers just to fill up space.**

# Ceramics

**Right** The deeply obscure Decatur Brewing Co. of Illinois produced this mug, with its attractive trademark of a bird carying malt and barley in its beak.

**Above** Three late 19th/early 20th century British pottery pint mugs, including in the middle one of the classic salmon-pink mugs loved by the writer George Orwell.

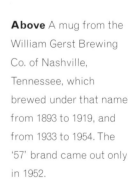

**Above** In the nineteenth century, customers would have beer delivered at home in stoneware gallon containers like this one from the English brewery Benskin's, with a brass tap at the front and a screwtop lid.

**Below** Another mug from a small brewer, K.G. Schmidt Brewing of Chicago.

**Below** Two pre-Prohibition American advertising mugs, one from Chicago's Franziskaner Brewing and Malting (a name that reflects one of Munich's most famous brews) and one from the Galland-Burke Brewing and Malting Co. of Spokane Falls, Washington, with a trademark of a hop leaf inside the brewer's six-pointed star.

**Above** A mug from the William Gerst Brewing Co. of Nashville, Tennessee, which brewed under that name from 1893 to 1919, and from 1933 to 1954. The '57' brand came out only in 1952.

**Below** Two mugs from Anheuser-Busch, each with a horse-racing theme.

**Below** Two attractive modern stoneware mugs, from the Budvar brewery in Ceske Budejovice, in the Czech Republic, and Tiger in Singapore. In the background is a mug from the former Benskin's brewery in Watford, just north of London, England, presented to brewery workers to mark the firm's centenary in 1967.

**Above** A lovely heavily-decorated 19th-century German beer stein.

**Above** The Independent Brewing Association of Chicago had this impressively Germanic stein made.

**Below** This more every-day European stein bears a decoration of fruit rather than anything connected with drinking.

# Ceramics – jugs

**Above** An early twentieth-century Bass water jug, made by Minton, England, which carries a clear statement of ownership on the base in an attempt to deter memorabilia collectors.

**Above** The acme of the steinmaker's art: any drinker would find it difficult to concentrate on the beer when confronted by naked women from handle to lid.

**Right** Two modern American steins, intended more for display at home than for actually drinking out of.

**Below** Two 1960s jugs from Mitchells & Butlers, the Birmingham, West Midlands, England, brewer and Offiler's of Derby, a couple of counties further north, which closed in 1966.

**Below** This simple earthenware glazed water jug, apparently issued by the London, England, brewer Barclay Perkins, is either a complete fake or a rare nineteenth-century example. It carries no maker's name and no other identification apart from the words 'Barclay's Stout.'

**Above and below** A pair of modern jugs from long-established English independent brewers, Brakspear's of Henley, in Oxfordshire, England, and the Suffolk, England, brewer Greene King.

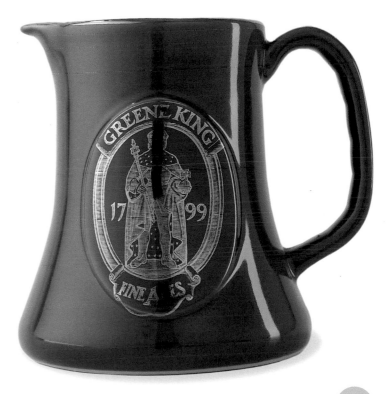

# Glass

**Above** The Glencoe Brewing Co. of Glencoe, Minnesota, which issued this etched glass, survived a disastrous fire in 1907 but could not survive Prohibition.

**Below** The Irish stout glass, as badged by Guinness with a 1950s poster showing the 'smiling pint.'

**Above** Two engraved glasses, a miniature mug and a lidded stein, all from Sioux Falls Brewing and Malting Co. of South Dakota, which closed in 1919.

**Below** Although the tulip-shape pint glass is most closely associated with stout, it is also used for serving ale, and this example carries a badge for Gladstone bitter, brewed by McMullen & Co. of Hertford, England.

**Above** A glass from Miller, with a horse-racing theme.

**Below** A variant on the tulip-shaped stout pint glass from Murphy's, the Cork brewery, which carries a traditional blessing in Irish: the words, in translation, begin: 'May the road rise up to meet you …'

**Left** The Aylesbury Brewery Company was a semi-independent arm of the giant Allied Breweries in Britain, and its trademark was the white Aylesbury farmyard duck.

**Right** A typical British 'dimple' pint glass badged with the Southwold Jack trademark of the Suffolk brewery Adnam's.

**Below** An American pint glass from Smuttynose Brewing of Portsmouth, New Hampshire.

**Below** The Waterford pint tankard given out by Guinness in the 1960s for serving its draft stout. Examples with the gold lettering undamaged are particularly hard to find. This is an early version, with pre-'hop sack' style lettering.

**Below** A plain pint glass almost identical to those in use today, but with a 'GR' excise stamp that shows it dates back to around World War I.

# Glass

**Left** Two attractive modern lager glasses, one badged by Beck's, the North German brewer, and the other from San Miguel, the company that started out in the Philippines and later reverse colonized Europe to become one of the biggest brewing companies in Spain.

**Below** A discreetly badged glass from the Mash brewery-restaurant just off Oxford Circus in the middle of London's West End, England.

**Above and below** Two tall, narrow badged lager glasses, one from the Prague brewery Staropramen (meaning 'old well') and the other from the Zaragozana brewery in Spain, advertising its *Ambar especial*.

**Above** Gillespie's is a Scottish stout revived in the early 1990s by Scottish and Newcastle Breweries, which has the original Gillespie, Sons & Co. brewery of Dumbarton, Strathclyde, which was closed in 1953, in its family tree.

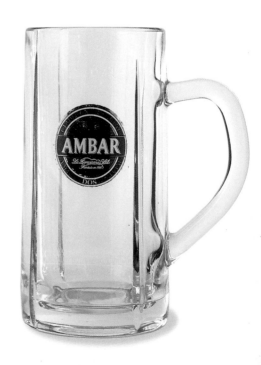

# Around the bar & on the table

The 'bar,' meaning the counter over which customers are served drinks and behind which staff perform their duties, entered the English language as a concept in the reign of Queen Elizabeth I, some 400 years ago. It was a bar or barrier between the public and private parts of the inn or tavern, often more like a serving hatch in a door than the bar counter we know today. Behind this barrier was the landlord's office and storeroom, which itself became known as 'the bar.' It was his private refuge, into which special guests and friends might be invited. Charles Dickens, in his novel *Barnaby Rudge*, described the looting of the Maypole Inn during the anti-Catholic Gordon Riots of 1780. The landlord, John Willett:

> 'Yes. Here was the bar – the bar that the boldest never entered without special invitation – the sanctuary, the mystery, the hallowed ground; here it was crammed with men, clubs, sticks, torches, pistols; filled with a deafening noise, oaths, shouts, screams, hootings; changed all at once into a bear-garden, a mad-house, an infernal temple; men darting in and out by door and window, smashing the glasses, turning the taps, drinking liquor out of china punchbowls, sitting astride casks, smoking private and personal pipes …wantonly wasting, breaking, pulling down and tearing up.'

Gradually the bar lost its exclusivity and the bar flap evolved into the bar counter, at least in larger establishments. At what period the bar counter became a regular item in drinking establishments is hard to say, partly because the bar has a more dominant or less dominant role depending on the precise nature of the institution, whether it is an inn, tavern, ale-house, gin-shop, pub, roadhouse, European-style café, or restaurant. An inventory of a London tavern, the King's Head in Leadenhall Street in 1627 includes: 'the Barr with the Bynnes [for wine] and three shelves …' as well as 'six drinking rooms with partitions…' One source says seventeenth-century taverns in America would generally have a bar. Contemporary illustrations of eighteenth-century alehouses, however, suggest that in these more humble places service was by waitress from the cask in the scullery. In many parts of the world,

Left **The Miller Girl toasts the highlife in the second half of the twentieth century.**

Germany for example, a waitress still brings your beer to your table. Even where the bar is found, waiters and waitresses can survive. There are pubs in the north of England, Scotland, and Ireland which preserve the bell pushes around the walls of the saloon bar used by customers to summon waitresses to take orders for drinks.

## DIFFERENT MEANINGS OF 'BAR'

Eventually the word 'bar' came to mean, especially in America, the whole of the premises serving drink and not just the counter behind which the drink was kept. In Britain, which preserved the idea of separate bars (public bar, saloon bar, and so on) within the same premises, the word still has the more restricted meaning of the pub's serving counter. Some pubs can still be found in rural parts of England which do not have any 'bar' at all, but preserve the idea of the pub as an ordinary house with a license to sell beer. Customers must go to the room where the beer is up on stillions (cask stands) to be supplied with drink. In these pubs, where the beat of life is still slow, and no one is in a rush to be served, the beer is served straight from the cask, with no pump. But urban life marches to a faster rhythm, and in the town the bar counter was found

Right **A tray from the Brakspear brewery, the Oxford family independent brewery.**

Left **An early twentieth-century match holder from the British brewer Ind Coope advertising its Burton ales.**

Right **A rare copper ashtray from the Oshkosh Brewing Co. of Oshkosh, Wisconsin.**

a necessity to speed up service and give staff a clear space in which to operate, and equally customers a place to stand and wait to be served. From the *Building News*, published in London, in 1857: 'Settles, or backed benches with a plank to each, sufficed in primitive times for the enjoyment of a cup of brown nappy with a pipe and a joke; the light of a coal fire, or the glimmer of a tallow fat illumed satisfactorily the boozy meetings of our ancestral artisans and swashbucklers; tonight it is otherwise – the corner public is radiant of gas, redolent of mahogany, and glittering in mirrors! There are no settles, no stools, nor any easy smoking with hard drinking … at the bar the droppers-in to drink must stand their treat, and move on when tired.'

However, some customers found the bar more congenial than waiter service. In 1909, the writer Frederick Hackwood complained that:

'At some establishments those old-time institutions, the "Bar" and the "Tap" are being abolished; and everywhere the employment of waiters, invariably looking for tips, is becoming more universal.'

## AN AREA RIPE FOR ADVERTISING

Once the bar had arrived, it was found to be essential for mounting the fonts and pumps for serving beer, to give a space for glasses to be placed in front of customers, and to protect the cash register. Photographs of nineteenth-century bars show them crowded with water jugs, siphon bottles, displays of sandwiches and pies under glass domes, salt and pepper pots, spirits urns, glasses, match strikers, wine coolers, ice buckets, mullers for tea and coffee, waiter trays, and ashtrays, even pot plants. Behind the bar, on what is still technically known as the stillion (from the days when it supported the casks of beer) were shelves for glasses and bottles, almost always with decorated mirrors behind. Shelf edges also bore their share of advertising materials, in card or flock.

Brewers have taken advantage of this space dedicated to the purchase of drink to advertise their products on font tap, on pump clip, and on mirror; and collectors have seized the opportunity to take these often very attractive objects home. The bar can be loaded with 'bar furniture,' from brightly lit fonts to bar towels, menu holders in china or metal, drinks trays, and so on. The back bar or stillion carries advertising figures, from Heileman's Rainier Beer Man in America to the red-capped Brewmaster of Flower's in Britain. Brewers have stamped their names on cutlery, plates, teapots and cups, condiment containers, cutlery holders, plastic sandwich markers, glass stands, siphon stands, and cigarette lighters, even plant pots.

There used to be brewery foam scrapers, but they are now outlawed as unhygienic in most countries where they were used, and there are even brewery can holders. Brewery clocks sit behind the bar, reminding drinkers of time's passage while they are having fun. Every table, in premises where you are still allowed to smoke, will carry an ashtray, often bearing a brewer's name or beer brand, which can be made from a raft of materials including brass,

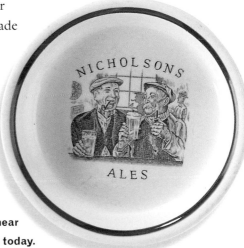

Right **A lovely China ashtray from Nicholson's of Maidenhead, England, in the 1940s or 1950s, depicting drinkers who would never be allowed near an advertising campaign today.**

copper, steel, glass, ceramics, and plastic. Tables are also the home for 'table tents,' folded-over cardboard (sometimes plastic) items advertising a particular beer.

In the United States, brewers produced tip trays on which drinkers could leave their gratuities. They also provided metal coasters, which had raised ribs to stop the glass or bottle sticking to them. These coasters were made from brass, steel, aluminum, or plastic. Some British brewers at the end of the nineteenth century issued ceramic coasters up to six inches in diameter, gorgeously decorated with multicolored illustrations showing brewery scenes, hops and barley, and bottle labels. Tthese are now extremely rare and, of course, correspondingly expensive.

The most heavily collected item of bar- or table-top beer memorabilia is probably the drinks tray, or – as many collectors prefer to call it – the waiter tray. Their size encouraged brewers to go for bold and striking designs, their inherent portability made them easy to remove from the premises, and their durability meant that far more trays have survived from early periods than probably any other type of bulky beer collectible.

The art of tray production, design, and printing reached its acme in pre-Prohibition America. The first printed metal trays were made by the Tuscarora Company, an advertising specialty manufacturer of Coshocton, Ohio, in 1895. Tuscarora merged with a rival firm, Standard Advertising, also of Coshocton in 1901 to form a new firm, Meek and Beach, which lasted only a few months before Mr Beach left to set up on his own again as the HD Beach Company. Meek and Beach then changed its name in 1909 to the American Art Works Company. This confusing

Above **Tap handles from the now-closed Narragansett brewery of Cranston, Rhode Island showing how a 'house style' can be used to great effect.**

narrative does have a benefit: it makes it easier to date pre-Prohibition waiter trays should they carry a manufacturer's name from any of these companies. However, another four or five companies in the United States also made waiter trays.

The earliest tin trays had anything up to ten or 20 different colors, which meant each raw tray had to go through the presses up to 20 times, drying off between runs. After that it was stamped, drawn into shape, and the lip curled over Photolithography, introduced in the 1900s, cut the number of colors that had to be used to four, and thus speeded up production dramatically, from fewer than 1,000 trays an hour to up to ten times that number.

Many of these early brewing trays showed idealized female beauties, often only semiclad in diaphanous costumes, with the brewery name as an afterthought. More usual subjects included bottles and glasses, brewery scenes and pictures of happy drinkers. One educational tray from the Hochstein brewery in Hudson, Wisconsin carried portraits of the first 24 presidents of the United States. All are regarded as hugely collectable, fetching large sums.

**US IS RICH IN OLD TRAYS**

Post-Prohibition trays are almost inevitably much plainer than those from before World War I. The same is true of trays from other parts of the world. In any case countries apart from the United States seem to have far fewer old trays surviving than are found within the US. In Britain, for example, most trays come from the early 1950s and later, with only a few pre-World War II ones known. But they are still popular with collectors, thanks to their bright strong designs. Most waiter trays are still made of metal, although some plastic ones have been seen.

The first patent for dispensing beer with carbon dioxide appeared in 1880. However, the wooden kegs then in use could not stand too much pressure, and it was a long time before gas dispense replaced the traditional manual beer engine. When Prohibition ended, and gas dispense became standard for draft beer in the United States, the law insisted that all beer taps should be marked with the name of the beer they were dispensing. Brewers therefore began distributing tap handles with their name on and, generally, a trademark or logo as well.

The earliest post-Prohibition tap handles or tap knobs were round. Later ones have been every shape imaginable. For example,

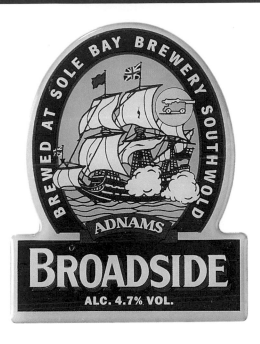

many look like miniature beer pump handles, both wooden and ceramic. Some look like little glasses of beer. Others have taken sport links: tap handles have been issued in the shape of baseballs, basketballs, golf balls on tees, bowling pins, and even surfboards and darts. Their size means that a collection of tap handles takes up little room, and they generally go for just a few dollars.

The British equivalent is the pump clip, the sign affixed to the traditional tall beer pump or beer engine handle to advertise the brew being dispensed. Although the handpump was in use from the beginning of the nineteenth century to bring up beer from the cellar, the pump clip is a later invention. Judging from old photographs they were unknown until the 1950s. The earliest pump clips were very plain, often in just two colors, and with no logo or trademark other than the brewer's name. The explosion in handpumped 'real ales' in Britain from the mid-1970s, and the growth in microbreweries that came with it, has meant a corresponding revolution in pump clip numbers and designs. Often the only way a small brewer can advertise the arrival of his beer in a new pub is via the pump clip, which is the first thing drinkers look at when they scan the bar. Early pump clips were made of plastic or, more rarely, enamel. Today they are found in pottery, metal, and wood, and with designs ranging from the amusing to the bizarre. Many collectors display their pump clips on wooden broom handles or similar-size pieces of pole, and they screw the pole to the wall using curtain rail brackets. Two linked collectable items, again peculiarly British, are the barrel bush, the

thick gun metal or brass ring that fits in the top of a wooden beer cask, where the 'shive,' the wooden plug goes to seal the contents; and the brass cask cellar tap. Barrel bushes in particular, and cask taps as well, are frequently stamped with the brewery's name. In the 1980s someone obtained the original dies used by one of Britain's biggest barrel bush makers, and a large number of fakes are now therefore in circulation.

## GOODBYE TO THE BAR TOWEL

One item of bar ware that appears to be vanishing is the bar towel, used to mop up spilt drink from the counter. Almost every brewery once issued these items to their pubs and they were normally made in cotton terry towelling, though they occasionally appeared in other absorbent materials. Most came in just two or three colors, with a simple logo or slogan. A very few microbrewers have issued bar towels, but they seem to be regarded as old-fashioned. It looks like the end to a fashion statement loved by some students: having a vest or jacket sewn up out of different brewers' towels.

In general, bar and table furniture is best picked up at collectors' fairs, flea markets, and junk and thrift shops. If you are friendly with a bar owner or manager, you may tap (pun intended) a regular source of handles or (in Britain) pump clips, which turn over quicker than items such as clocks or cutlery. There are a few specific clubs around the world specializing in bar 'furniture,' and you are also likely to meet fellow collectors through other clubs.

# Trays

**Above** The six-pointed star featured on the waiter tray from the J. Leisy Brewing Co. of Cleveland, Ohio, is the alchemist's symbol for the unity of the four 'elements,' earth, air, fire, and water, which has been used by brewers since the thirteenth century.

**Above** A waiter tray in the style known as 'pie-plate' from the Christian Moerlein brewery in Cincinnati, which closed in 1919.

**Left** Food was a popular subject for waiter tray illustrations, and this lobster-led extravaganza from the John Hohenadel Brewery of Philadelphia, which closed in 1953, is a fine example.

**Right** A superb brewery scene on a pre-Prohibition tray from the Indianapolis Brewing Co. Its Duesseldorfer beer, one of four advertised around the edge of the tray, won top prize at the Louisiana Purchase Exposition in St Louis in 1904.

**Top and above** Two trays bearing the name of the
Bartels Brewing Company, which ran separate breweries
in Edwardsville, Pennsylvania and Syracuse, New York.
The young woman appears to be suffering from a broken
neck, but is smiling gamely on. The seventeenth-century
figure holding the giant mug is a variant of the
'Professor' who appeared in much of the company's
advertising. The Syracuse brewery closed in 1942, the
Edwardsville one in 1968, though the brand survived in
the hands of Lion Brewing of Wilkes-Barre.

# Trays, towels & match holders

A selection of five metal waiter trays, made in the 1950s and early 1960s, from English brewers. Of the round trays, one is a visual pun from the London brewer Fuller Smith and Turner and one is a golden statement from a Yorkshire brewery which also brewed its last in 1968. The square and rectangular trays show different approaches to filling the medium. The comprehensive branding, by the Stroud brewery in Gloucestershire, which even plugs the local tourist attractions and the popularity of its beers with both sexes; the single tempting glass from Barclay's; and the cheery old gaffer from Magee, Marshall and Co. of Bolton, Lancashire, England.

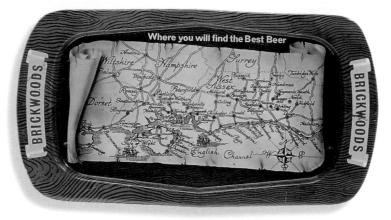

## THROWING IN THE TOWEL

Bar towels are getting to be a thing of the past. Here are two by two vanished English brewers, Brickwood's of Portsmouth, on the south coast of England, and Beverley's of Wakefield, West Yorkshire, England, another 1960s casualty.

**Above** Bimini, advertised on this late 19th-century match striker, was one of several brands produced by the Reisch brewery in Springfield, Illinois. The brewery was founded in 1849 and closed in 1966.

**Above** This odd-looking object is a cola syrup dispenser used by Stroh's of Detroit during the Prohibition years in a bid to build a soft drink brand to rival Coca-cola. It was not a success, and was withdrawn.

# Ashtrays

**Above** Four ashtrays from vanished English breweries: West Country, which went under in the early 1960s; Gray's of Essex, which closed in 1974; Higson's, the Liverpool brewer, which shut down in 1990; and Almond's of Standish in Lancashire, a tiny brewery with just 16 pubs which was taken over in 1968.

**Above** Ashtrays in various materials from different English brewers: a colored glass ashtray by Wells & Winch of Biggleswade from before 1961; a steel example put out under the name of a vanished brewer, Benskin's of Watford, in the 1980s by the Allied Brewers concern.

**Above** A plain, shield-shape ashtray from the White Shield brewery, England.

**Below** A pair of 'label' ashtrays issued by English brewers in the 1950s, one from Daniell's of Colchester, Essex, and the other by Friary's of Guildford, Surrey.

**AROUND THE BRITISH ISLES**

Five ashtrays from around the British Isles, all 1970s and 1980s: a giant metal one from Bass Ulster, in Belfast, Northern Ireland; a green glass for Banks's Mild from the West Midlands; china for Ind Coope's Burton Ale; plastic for the Welsh brewer Brain's; and clear glass for the microbrewer Banks & Taylor of Shefford, in Bedfordshire.

# Pump taps & clips

## PENNSYLVANIAN TAP KNOBS

A selection of aluminum tap knobs culled solely from western Pennsylvania, showing the variety to be found in just one small area.

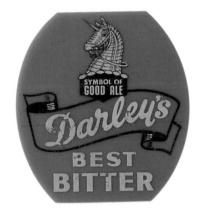

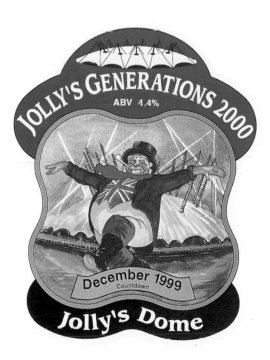

**Above** In the top of wooden beer casks are screwed metal rings called barrel bushes, which are sealed with a wooden 'shive' or bung when the cask is filled. British brewers generally had their names cast into the barrel bushes: the three loose ones are from two still existing brewers, Wadworth's and Young's, and one which vanished in 1969, Strong's of Romsey, in Hampshire. The fourth is a rare example more than 50 years old from the time when Guinness came in wooden casks, which has been made into an ashtray using oak that may be from a beer cask too.

**Above** Three small, comparatively plain pump-handle clips from the 1950s and 1960s from the Yorkshire brewer Darley's of Thorne, Nottinghamshire's James Hole & Co. of Newark and Benskin's of Watford, England.

**Above** In 1999 the Lincolnshire brewer Bateman's brought out a different beer every month celebrating a different event in the preceding millennium. Each beer had its own special pump clip. These two are for July, which celebrated the first moon landing, and December, which celebrated the Millennium Dome at Greenwich.

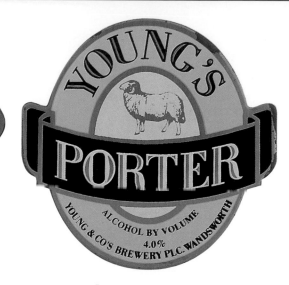

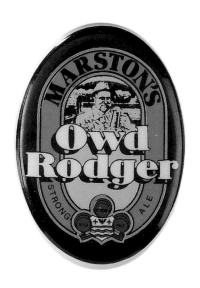

**Left** Brewers generally try to make their pump clip designs match, as in these pairs from the 1980s: Greene King for its dark mild and its strong Abbot Ale; and the Burton brewer Marston's for Merrie Monk, a strong mild, and Owd Roger, a strong 'Burton' ale. The other pump clips featured come from Taylor Walker, a subsidiary of the former British brewing giant Allied Breweries; Fuller, Smith & Turner and Young's, two London brewers; Brains, whose clips echo the style of rugby shirts; and the Leeds, Yorkshire brewer Tetley.

## STATUE COLLECTION

**Above** When Carling, the Canadian lager brand, began brewing in the United States in the 1950s one of the novelty items it used to promote itself was this almost two-foot-high cardboard barn. The electrically powered dancers actually move …

**Above** Statuettes of the Miller High Life girl, like this one, were familiar sights in American bars during the early 1950s.

**Right** Falstaff figures come in considerable variety, reflecting the beer's one-time wide production: the Falstaff Brewing Corporation had eight plants around the United States in the early 1970s, from Rhode Island through California. The brand's roots lie in the Wm. J. Lemp Brewing Co. of St Louis, Missouri. The Falstaff name was bought from Lemp in 1920 by Joseph Griesedieck, who set up the Falstaff Beverage Co. When Prohibition ended this had become the Falstaff Brewing Corp.

**Right** The brewery worker with the wooden barrel on his shoulder was issued by Poth Brewing of Philadelphia in the mid-1930s.

# Back bar

**Above** A good example of cardboard back-bar display from the John Hauenstein brewery of New Ulm, Minnesota, founded in 1864 and closed in 1970.

**Above** It was probably a long time since Goebel of Detroit used wooden barrels, but the image gave some class to its Private Stock 22 brand.

**Above** Few brewery clocks are as elaborate as this one from Kolb Brothers Brewing of West Bay City (now part of Bay City), Michigan. The brewery ran from 1867 to 1939.

**Above** A lovely 'chalk' (the term for back-bar displays made from plaster of Paris) issued by Schell's of New Ulm, Minnesota, almost certainly before 1920.

**Below** Two back bar 'chalks' with horsy themes. One is from the early 1950s by Hudepohl of Cincinnati, Ohio. The other is from Falls City of Louiseville, Kentucky, probably made in the early 1970s—the brewery closed in 1978.

**Above** The beer-drinking armadillo was issued by Lone Star of San Antonio, Texas to bars taking its beers in the late 1950s. Lone Star was taken over by Heileman in 1983, 99 years fter it was founded..

# Gifts & goodies

If it can have a name printed on it, you can bet some brewer somewhere has had it branded and given it away to customers as an advertising gimmick. Sewing-kits, shoehorns, manicure sets (including toenail clippers), computer mouse mats, fans, fountain pens, flashlights, pocket watches, pencils, penknives, notebooks, diaries, badges, cufflinks, and cuddly toys, even oven mitts and pot holders, are some of the unusual items that have borne brewery names.

Objects with more obvious connections with bars and taverns that have made it as brewery collectibles by virtue of carrying the brand name of a beer or brewer include bottle openers, can openers, corkscrews, cigarette lighters, cigar cutters, match safes, matchbooks and matchboxes, dart flights, tobacco boxes, decks of cards, cribbage boards, bottle and can coolers, and 'free beer' tokens. Corkscrews often come as part of a combined penknife-and-corkscrew set. Combined keyrings and bottle openers are very popular; beer-branded plain keyrings are also known. Some brewers have given away keyring 'charms.' The British brewer Watney handed out thousands of little red plastic barrels (its trademark) with a metal loop to fit onto a keyring, while its fellow British brewer McMullen's gave away 'lucky' horseshoe charms branded with the name of its bottled pale ale, Mac's Number 1.

Sporty giveaways and goodies include baseballs, baseball bats, and baseball mitts branded with brewers' names; golf tees and golf balls; scorekeepers, and match schedules printed with the brewers' names; and team shirts bearing the name of a brewery sponsor.

## CLOTHING HAS IT COVERED
Clothing covers a huge area of beer memorabilia goodies: the Firkin chain of brewpubs in Britain, by virtue of its largely student

Right **One of the oddest brewery giveaways ever, this 30-pound 16-inch diameter weight from the Lone Star brewery in San Antonio, Texas, was for hitching your horse to when there was no fence or post available ...**

clientele, found a market for brewery-branded socks and underwear. T-shirts are the biggest area in brewery-branded clothing, and even the tiniest microbrewer will often have his (or her) own T-shirt or sweatshirt for sale with the brewery name or logo on the front. (Not always on the front, however: the Australian brewer who makes Redback beer, named for a local venomous spider, puts the logo, naturally enough, on the T-shirt back.) There is a dilemma here however. Collectibles are always more valuable when unused, but the fun of a brewery T-shirt is wearing it. And it's even better if the shirt you're wearing is for a beer unknown in your part of the world. Perhaps the answer is always to buy two, one for wearing and one for collecting…

Neckties are also popular. Brewers have always had neckties made for their own staff, and they often give them away to favored bar owners and customers. The biggest brewery necktie collections number hundreds, and Dublin airport has a stand devoted to selling Guinness neckties carrying a changing range of designs.

Other items of branded clothing include hats, sweaters, shirts with a brewery name embroidered on the shirt pocket, sweatshirts, and jackets. Often brewers will have special promotional offers for items such as baseball jackets, where tokens need to be collected off can or bottle packs, then a set number of these are sent off with money to obtain the desired piece of clothing. Sometimes the branding is very subtle. For example the German brewer Holsten sold a black leather-and-cloth jacket in the mid-1990s with the brewery's 'Ritter' trademark embroidered in black on the back, and the silk quilted lining was in the same shade of green as the foil around the Holsten Pils bottle necks.

The first brewery giveaways were probably calendars bearing the brewery name and a picture of a beautiful young woman. At the Chicago Fair of 1893, more properly the World's Columbian Exposition, a row marred the preopening flurries of the event when one of the organizers, Mrs Potter Palmer, objected to her photograph appearing on calendars issued by some of the 24 brewers at the fair. The brewers, however, responded that,

'as an official of the World's Columbian Exposition of so distinguished merit and accomplishment, she has become also a distinguished individual, and her face and fame a public possession. Greatness is death to privacy, and a distinguished success pays the penalty in publicity.'

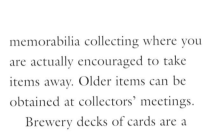

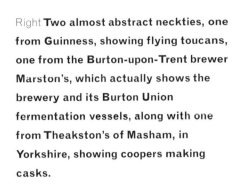

Right **Two almost abstract neckties, one from Guinness, showing flying toucans, one from the Burton-upon-Trent brewer Marston's, which actually shows the brewery and its Burton Union fermentation vessels, along with one from Theakston's of Masham, in Yorkshire, showing coopers making casks.**

Today, calendars showing young ladies in states of considerable undress issued by American breweries at the turn of the twentieth century sell for four-figure sums. You can find considerably cheaper brewery calendars from the 1960s at collectors' fairs and the like. These will normally be one-day-to-a-sheet calendars made of cardboard-backed tin, with two hooks for the calendar pad.

Calendars were followed by matchbooks, or matchcovers as collectors like to call them, and match boxes. Few established brewers have not issued matches at some time, and since matchbooks and matchboxes generally have long been collectibles, beer-branded ones turn up quite often at collectors' fairs, flea markets, and so on. The biggest collections number about 3,500 different boxes and books, all beery, and from all around the world. Incidentally, the other great collecting hobby, philately, has thrown up very few beery collectibles. There are just two examples. First, Arthur Guinness appeared on a stamp issued in Ireland in the 1950s, and then in 1995 France issued a stamp showing the maltings attached to the old brewery at Stenay in Lorraine.

### THE 'SKEDDER CHAPTER'

For many years, American brewers have printed team-game schedules, known as 'skeds' on everything from beer cans through keyrings, to let fans know when and where their teams will be playing each season. The Beer Can Collectors of America has a 'skedder chapter.' Schedules have also appeared on plastic cups used for beer at ballgames, on coasters, on table tents, on refrigerator magnets and on pens, as well as on big bar posters and the most usual wallet-size 'pocket schedule.' More than 12,000 different pocket schedules sponsored by brewers are known, and there are at least 200 different schedules printed on cans. Collectors get most of their new material for free from bars and ballparks. Indeed, this is one of the very few areas of beer

memorabilia collecting where you are actually encouraged to take items away. Older items can be obtained at collectors' meetings.

Brewery decks of cards are a collecting field of their own, although collectors are split between those who are only interested in the back sides, the side that normally carries the branding, and those who prefer the full deck. 'Full deckers' point out that often the ace of spades carries special branding on the front, while sometimes brewers have made every card different. (The arms of the Worshipful Company of Cardmakers in Britain, incidentally, includes a red lion, which had been suggested as one reason why so many British pubs are called the Red Lion!) Several hundred different sets of brewery decks of cards are known, and again they often appear at collectors' fairs.

Brewery tokens have attracted specialist collectors. Most are giveaways entitling the bearer to a free drink, although in times when small change was short – such as in 1860s' America during the Civil War – brewers issued their own coins to try to cope. Paper fans issued and branded by brewers were popular in pre-Prohibition America and also in 1950s' France

British brewers, particularly microbrewers, seem keen to celebrate alternative drinks! A large number of coffee mugs and teacups bearing brewery logos have been issued in the past 20 years, gathering their own specialist collectors. Other minority areas include pencils advertising breweries and beers, of which nearly 200 are known. There is even one pencil with a bottle opener on the end!

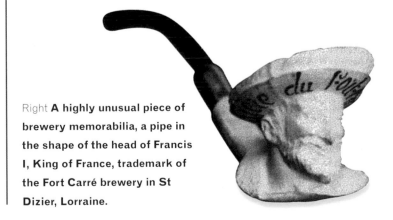

Right **A highly unusual piece of brewery memorabilia, a pipe in the shape of the head of Francis I, King of France, trademark of the Fort Carré brewery in St Dizier, Lorraine.**

# Gifts & goodies

**Above** A miniature mug from the pre-pro Grand Falls brewery.

**Above** A button and watch fob for Ambrosia lager by the Sioux Falls Brewing and Malting Co. of South Dakota, which closed in 1919 after 45 years of brewing.

**Left** A rare cork puller from Crystal Export Lager, Michigan.

**Above** A bottle stopper in the shape of the Hawaiian chieftain trademark used on Primo brand beer which was brewed in Honolulu until 1979, when the brewery closed.

**Above** Brewery patches were generally for sewing on to the overalls of brewery workers. Fox Head closed in 1962.

**Right** Open the lid on this cardboard stein and up pop a happy couple. The brewery in Worcester, Massachusetts, finally closed in 1962.

**Above** In the list of odd brewery giveaways, this pre-Prohibition spoon from Sioux Falls Brewing of South Dakota, with an engraving of the brewery in the bowl, ranks high.

**Below** Two model trucks bearing brewers' logos, one the long-established family brewery Fuller Smith and Turner of London, England, and the other the Scottish microbrewery Isle of Skye: the inscription in Gaelic means 'Beer of the Island.'

**Above** Brewery neckties from around the British Isles: the Welsh brewery Felinfoel, the Firkin brewpub chain, Ringwood, the microbrewery in Hampshire founded in 1978 by Peter Austin, who was the 'father' of the British microbrewery revolution, and the Castletown brewery on the Isle of Man, which closed in 1986.

**Left** An Australian necktie, from Cooper's brewery in Adelaide, with three British examples from vanished breweries, Matthew Brown of the Lion brewery, Blackburn, taken over in 1987, Watney's, whose Thameside brewery now brews Budweiser for the UK market, and Flower's, taken over in 1961, which inherited the red-hatted Brewmaster figure from JW Green.

**Above** Two buttons from former Chicago breweries, one showing the 'YUSAY' trademark registered by the Pilsen Brewing Co. (closed 1963) after it was refused permission to use the straightforward 'USA,' and the other from Ambrosia, whose Nectar brand came in cans as well, which ran from 1938 to 1959.

**Below** An unusual miniature flashlight bearing the name of ESB, the strong bitter brewed by Fuller Smith and Turner of London, England, which spawned many imitators among American microbrewers.

# Gifts & goodies

**Above** A zip-up foam fabric bottle-cooler from the Holsten brewery in Germany, ideal for the beach.

**Right** A raft of tiny 'giveaway' collectibles including 1970s badges from two English real ale breweries, Ridley's of Essex and Rayment's of Hertfordshire; a 'free pint' token from Theakston's, the Yorkshire brewer; several varieties of Guinness lapel badges, together with a Guinness tiepin and cufflink set; a minute and discreet 'red triangle' badge from Bass; a 1960s' Red Barrel keyring charm from Watney's; a lapel badges for AK, a beer brewed by the south of England brewer McMullen's; and a pair of cufflinks from the 1930s issued by the Ancient Order of Froth Blowers, an English social club and charity fund raising organisation.

**Left and Right** Bourne Valley, a south of England microbrewery which closed in 1985, had time to produce a coffee mug for customers before it stopped brewing. Bass, the huge Burton upon Trent-based brewing concern, preferred putting its logo on something more suitable for tea.

**Left** An electrically powered clock issued by Charles Wells, the brewer of Bedford, England, issued to celebrate the firm's 100th anniversary. These clocks would have been given out to suppliers and wholesalers, as well as the brewery's own pubs.

**Right** Matchboxes, still along with matchbooks in many countries the commonest brewery giveaway, are represented by a lone American, Union Station brewery, brewer of Golden Spike ale, from the capital of Rhode Island. There are several British examples, including one from the Firkin brewpub chain, and a 1950s' box from the little Hertfordshire brewery Rayment's, as well as a modern Heineken box distributed in the UK.

**Below** Coffee mugs from two family breweries in England's West Country, Gibbs Mew (now closed) and Hall & Woodhouse of Dorset, which still brews its Badger beers.

**Below** Coffee mugs from Harvey's of Sussex, in the south of England, carry an attractive line drawing of the nineteenth-century brewery, while Caledonian, an independent brewery from Edinburgh, Scotland, goes for a stylish blue-on-gold design.

**Below** This briefcase, made out of sheets of unformed Holsten beer cans, was part of a press kit giveaway in the early 1990s, and was originally filled with bottles of beer.

**Above** A fan given away by the French brewery Brasserie Tourtel of Tantonville in the 1930s. Tourtel survives today only as the name of an alcohol-free beer.

**Above** A tin box given away by Holsten free when you bought a bottle of the beer in the mid-1990s, is covered in designs meant to emphasize the brand's 'export' attributes.

# Shirts

**Top** A T-shirt from Willett's brewpub in Napa, California, which changed its name to Downtown Joe's in the early 1990s; the Dublin Brewery Company claims to be the second-biggest brewer in Ireland's capital – second to Guinness, that is.
**Middle** Gillespie's is a Scottish stout that revives the name of an old brewery which vanished around 50 years ago; Alpirsbacher is an abbey brewery in Germany, and its Dunkel is the dark version of a wheat beer.
**Bottom** This embroidered sweatshirt with the Bacchus trademark comes from the Hopback brewery in Salisbury, England; an Australian T-shirt advertising Foster's low-alcohol Special Bitter, a beer designed to let drinkers consume as much beer, with less effect.

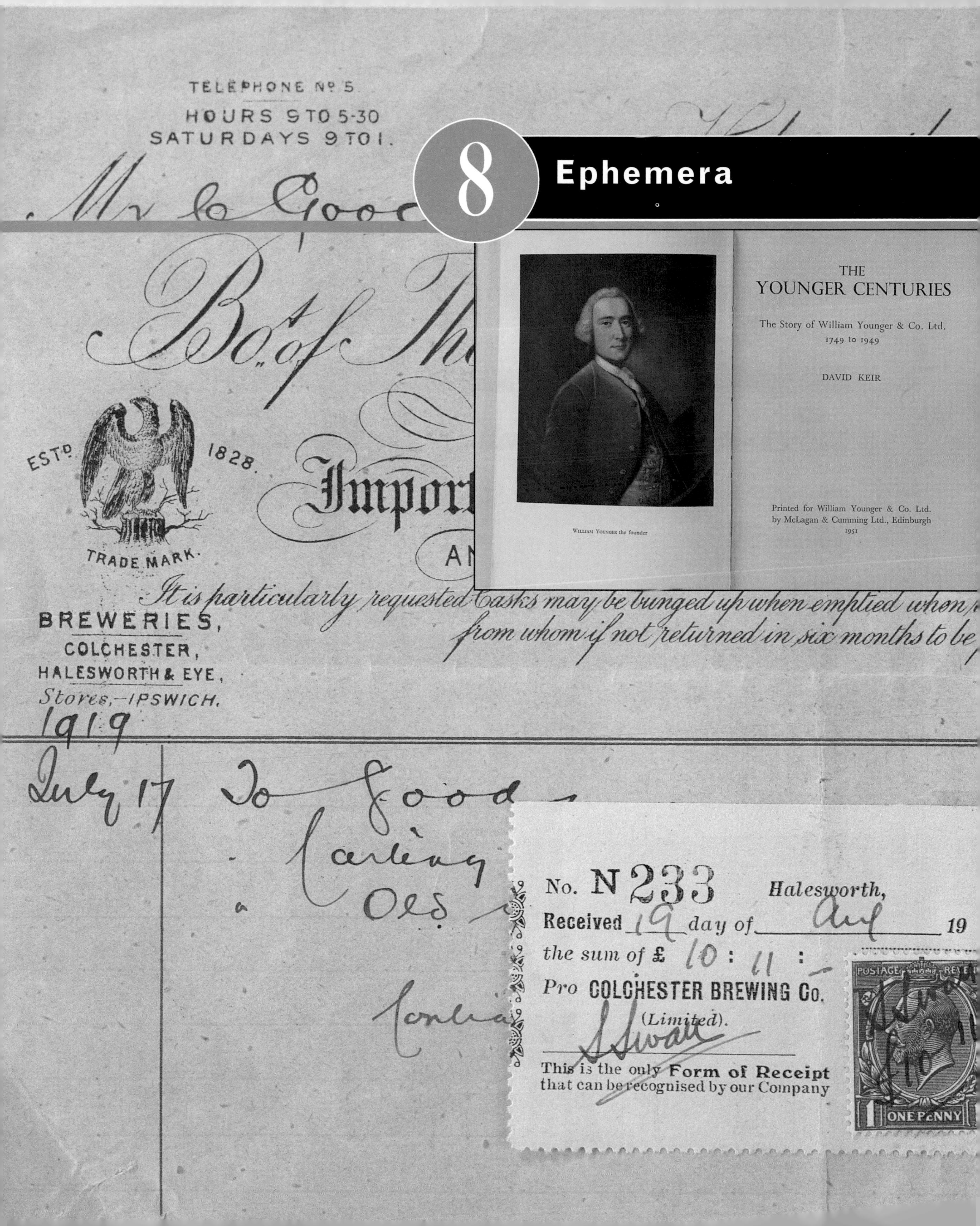

TELEPHONE No. 5.
HOURS 9 TO 5-30
SATURDAYS 9 TO 1.

*Mr & Good*

*B. of The*

ESTD. 1828.

TRADE MARK.

*Import*

AN

It is particularly requested Casks may be bunged up when emptied when
from whom if not returned in six months to be

**BREWERIES,**
COLCHESTER,
HALESWORTH & EYE,
Stores.—IPSWICH.

*1919*

*July 17   To Good*

*Carting*

*Old*

THE
YOUNGER CENTURIES

The Story of William Younger & Co. Ltd.
1749 to 1949

DAVID KEIR

WILLIAM YOUNGER the founder

Printed for William Younger & Co. Ltd.
by McLagan & Cumming Ltd., Edinburgh
1951

No. **N 233**   Halesworth,
Received *19* day of *Aug*   19
the sum of £ *10 : 11 : —*
Pro **COLCHESTER BREWING Co.**
(Limited).

*S Swan*

This is the only **Form of Receipt**
that can be recognised by our Company

POSTAGE REVE

ONE PENNY

# Ephemera

**E**phemera is throwaway stuff, items that would normally end up in the trash can, yesterday's garbage. Breweries, bars, and beer generate plenty of ephemera, including bills, letterheads, price lists, and the like. In Germany there are specialist collectors of *kellnerzettel*, the bills the waiter brings you after an evening in the bar, which are normally decorated with advertising material for the bar in question – bits of paper that most people would crumple up and toss into the gutter. For collectors of ephemera there is something almost guilty about hoarding stuff that most other people would regard as trash. At the same time there is a feeling that you are doing a worthy job; if someone doesn't collect this stuff, it will be lost for ever.

The great English collector Robert Opie, who has made a career of hoarding every kind of packaging, says he first started collecting such items as a child when he ate a chocolate bar and was about to throw the wrapper away. Suddenly he realized that if all the wrappers were only ever thrown away, there would be nothing to show the world in future times what a chocolate bar wrapper looked like. Opie was also probably influenced by his parents, Peter and Iona Opie, who were recorders of children's playground songs and games, ephemeral activities that would,

Right **A union banner from the St Paul chapter of the United Brewery Workmen of American Union.**

again, vanish beyond recall if someone did not deliberately and systematically collect them. Today we are fascinated to see the few surviving bits of paper our grandparents and great-grandparents kept; partly because it reminds us of different times, partly because so little of it has survived. The collectors of ephemera can know that future historians will be very grateful to them.

## A HUGE RANGE OF COLLECTABLE ITEMS

'Ephemera' is actually the plural of the little-used word ephemeron, which comes from the Greek word, *ephemeros*, meaning 'lasting only a day,' and in biology it is used as the generic term for mayflies and other insects with a short lifespan. The eighteenth-century writer Dr Samuel Johnson (whose head was used as a trademark by the London brewer Barclay Perkins) was one of the first people to use the word in something close to the sense that collectors give it, of items that are generally thrown away after a short time, when he spoke of 'these papers of a day, the Ephemerae of learning.'

Today 'ephemera' covers a huge range of collectable items. Old brewery bills, for example, are frequently fascinating because often they carried a finely engraved 'billhead' showing the brewery

premises. Sometimes they even carried color representations of the brewery's bottle labels. These historical documents can be found very cheaply at ephemera fairs. They often come via lawyers' offices, when clearouts are made of old documents relating to long-dead clients' estates. Other old brewery documents sought by collectors include price lists, and brewery share certificates.

Postcards and trade cards are another collecting area with big possibilities. Trade cards were distributed by breweries in the United States from the 1880s, usually showing a bottle of beer or three, sometimes posed in incongruous situations, such as next to a vase of roses. Brewers also distributed postcard photographs of their breweries. In Germany, brewers printed postcards carrying the brewery name, a cartoon of drinkers enjoying the product, leaving room for a ribald message from the sender. Britain had a huge postcard boom in the first decade of the twentieth century and, while few surviving cards show pictures of breweries, many show pubs carrying brewers' signboards. Genuine photographs of old breweries also turn up sometimes, as do prints and engravings. Old newspapers often carry advertisements from brewers, as do old magazines, and both make fascinating collectables. However preservation is a problem, as it is with all paper-based ephemera. Because, by definition, these items were never expected to last, the

Above **Cases for bottles were often chopped up, burnt, or otherwise destroyed, and few survive, though they often carried terrific designs on the sides, as with this example from South Falls Brewing of South Dakota. The brewery closed in 1919.**

materials were the cheapest that could be used. Paper and card packaging, again normally thrown away, is often colorful and collectable. In the United States some people collect 'beer bags,' the paper shopping bags designed to carry bottles home from the package store, which carried brewers' logos and artwork showing the bottles. These were made obsolete by the cardboard six-pack, and six-pack cartons themselves (and the earlier two-pack and four-pack cartons) have their collectors. Many brewers now produce promotional plastic carrier bags with their names on, and you can bet someone is collecting them too!

### SAVED FROM THE TRASH CAN

Lots of other paper brewery ephemera survives only because someone puts it in a drawer or cupboard rather than the trash can. Included are promotional leaflets for new beers, throwaway guides to brewery visits, even paper tray covers for beer sampling – all end up in collections.

While not strictly ephemera, books about beer, brewing, and breweries are very collectable, and even the reprints of the rarer books are now hard to find. For example the classic *Curiosities of Ale and Beer*, written in 1886 by the journalist Charles Henry Cook under the pseudonym John Bickerdyke, is quoted in almost every modern book about beer, and is thus almost impossible to get hold of.

There are also collectors of beery music: the Beer Song Collectors of America meets once a year during the annual 'canvention' of the Beer Can Collectors of America. It is traditional for the meeting to start at 3.33⅓ in the afternoon. Beery music need not be restricted to pop songs, however. The Scottish brewer Tennents sponsored a recording of specially written traditional-style Scottish airs to celebrate the centenary of lager brewing in Scotland, now a very rare LP.

Below **A stock certificate from the 1950s for Fox Head Brewing of Waukesha, Wisconsin. The brewery was taken over and closed by G. Heileman of LaCrosse, Wisconsin, in 1962, although the brand lived on.**

# Ephemera

**Left and below** The cover of a price list from the 1890s by Salters of Rickmansworth, Herfordshire, England, showing the 'covered wagon' form of brewer's dray used by English country brewers at the time.

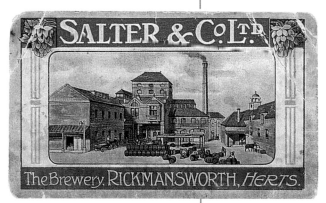

**Right** A fine postcard from the Sioux Falls Brewing Company of South Dakota, promoting its lager: the company lasted just one year after Prohibition ended.

**Above** The beautiful colored card price-list inside, showing the huge range of draft beers typical of the variety available to Victorian beer drinkers, with only a couple of bottled beers on sale.

**Right** A set of five pre-World War II bottle openers from Britain. Allsopp's, which merged with Ind Coope in 1934, was one of Burton-upon-Trent's giants, Taylor Walker was one of London's biggest former brewers, Wrexham was a small lager-only brewer in north Wales, while Phillips was a little family brewery in Stamford, Lincolnshire, and Praed's (properly Campbell Praed's) was another in Wellingborough, Northamptonshire.

**Below** A New Year's card from 1883 when the concern Bernard Stroh founded in 1850 was still known as the Lion Brewing Co., opened out to show the complete design. Tivoli beer was later renamed Bohemian beer.

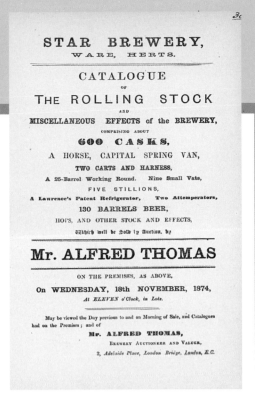

**Above** A rare auction catalog from the 1870s for the fittings of a little English country brewery, the sort of item that sometimes turns up at ephemera fairs.

**Above** Before World War I the Hull Brewery Co of East Yorkshire issued these lovely receipts illustrated with examples of the company's bottle labels.

**Above** The White Horse, one of the few tied houses belonging to Well's brewery of Watford, England, issued this illustrated receipt in the middle of World War I.

**Below** A long-playing record from the 1970s issued by Britain's National Youth Jazz Orchestra celebrating some of the country's best-known real ale breweries: the photograph was taken in the yard of Young's brewery in London. Tracks on the LP included *Young's Makes Me Feel You So*, and *That Old Peculier Feeling*.

**Above** A receipt issued in 1919 by the Colchester Brewing Company of Essex, England, nicely illustrated with the company trademark and instructions about 'bunging up' returned casks.

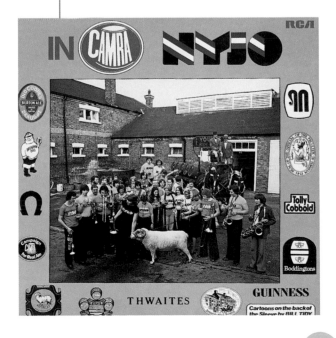

# Books

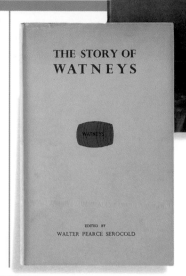

**Left and below** *The Barley and the Stream*, a scholarly history of Canada's oldest brewery company, Molson's, published in 1955, has been a source for several general books on brewing history.

**Above** The English writer Richard Boston wrote a highly influential book in 1976 which helped educate Britain's beer drinkers on the heritage around them. Copies are now hard to find because most original buyers have kept theirs.

**Above** Two books on London, England, brewers that later merged, one published 1949 and the other 1966. Both, like all the best books on brewery history, are packed with great old photographs and fascinating anecdotes.

**Bottom row** Although written a half century ago, this is still a very collectable volume on the history of one of Scotland's premier breweries.

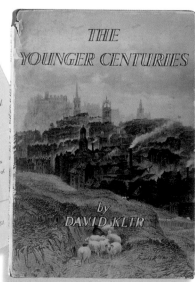

# 9 Specialist collections

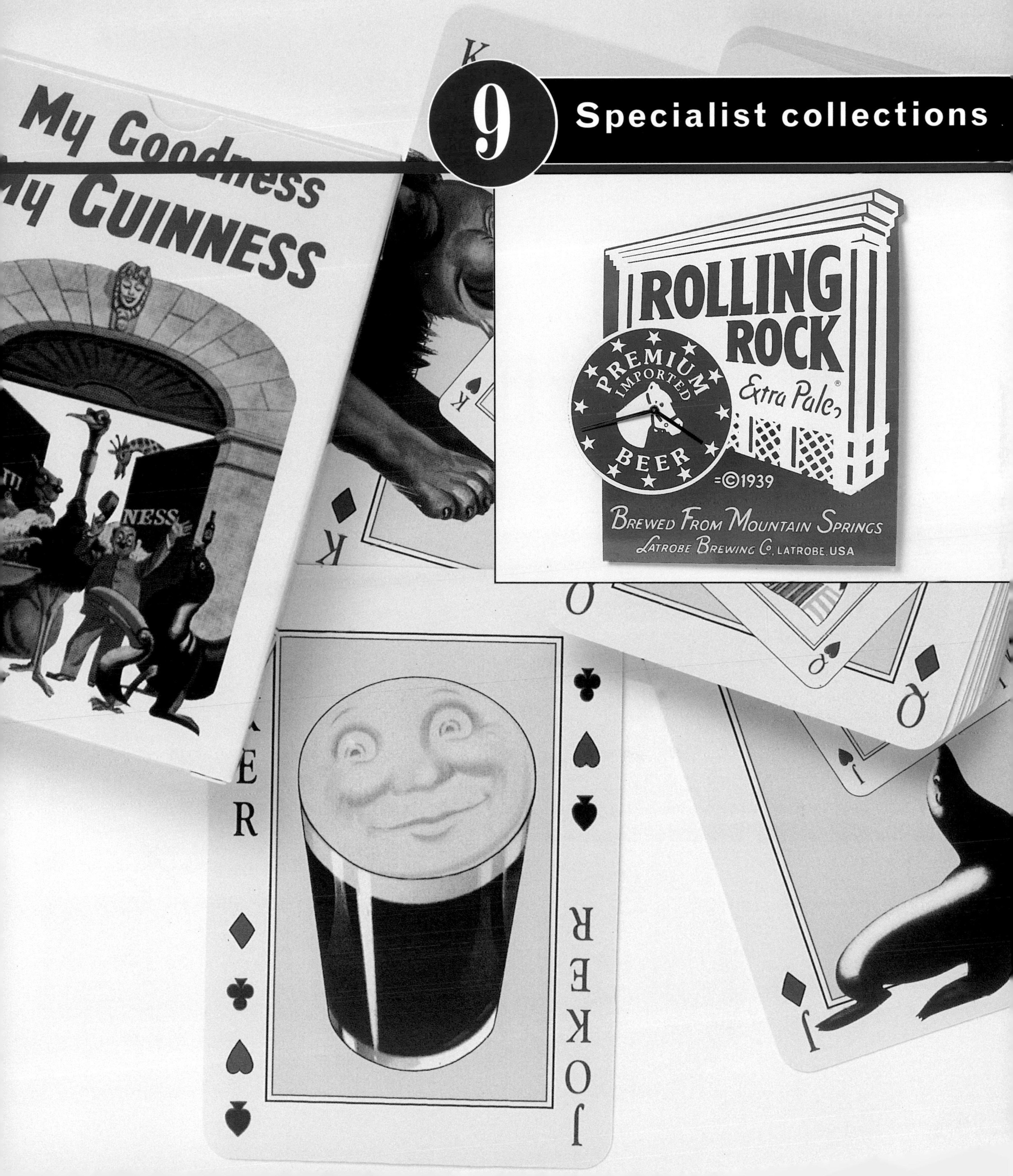

# Specialist collections

## BILLINGS

For collectors looking to concentrate on just one brewery, if they live locally to a concern like the Billings Brewing Co. of Billings, Montana, they are in luck. Billings produced a variety of collectables, pre- and post-Prohibition, from waiter trays through ashtrays, cone-top cans through neon signs.

Work on building the brewing began in late 1899, at a cost of $100,000, and the first bottles of Old Fashion brand beer were bottled the following May. The brewery was quickly using the slogan 'The Beer that Made Milwaukee Jealous,' and promoting Old Fashion with a car shaped and painted in order to resemble a beer bottle.

The temperance movement triumphed in Montana in 1918, and in February the following year Billings; brewery workers had to pour beer worth $12,000 down the drain. During the 'dry' years the company made soda, but in 1933 it leapt back into action, brewing almost 4,500 barrels of beer up to December 31. The company neglected the brewery equipment, however, and high production costs meant that for a while it was making a loss.

A new brand, Billings Pale, introduced in 1940, helped push the company back into profit, but the profits were used to pay dividends and debts, and the brewing equipment continued to deteriorate. By 1947 Old Fashion was so bad it was almost undrinkable, and thousands of gallons had to be poured away. A new canning line in 1950 failed to stop the rot: by now Old Fashion, which was sold in a green can, was known to drinkers as 'green death.' Another new brand, Billings Tap, was introduced in the summer of 1951, but although it was favorably received, Billings found itself unable to throw off the bad reputation of Old Fashion.

In December 1951 Billings' stockholders, faced with the choice of spending money to replace antique brewing equipment or shutting the brewery entirely, plumped for closure. The brewery remained empty until 1959, when it was demolished.

**Above** An illuminated sign for Billings' Old Fashion beer.

**Right** A pre-Prohibition 'American Beauty' waiter tray with the slogan 'The Beer that Made Milwaukee Jealous.'

**Above** A glass sign for the short-lived Tap brand.

**Right** Two glass signs for Old Fashion, one more 'select' than the other.

**Above** An enchanting 1920s ceramic coaster featuring bathing beauties on the diving board.

**Above** Another pre-Prohibition waiter tray, this time featuring a local landmark, the Lower Yellowstone Falls.

### ONE TOWN – HUDSON

Almost any town can supply enough material for a specialist collection, and Hudson, New York, is a good example, even though its two breweries closed early in the twentieth century. Brewing started in Hudson in 1788 (or 1786 according to some accounts) when William Faulkner, a New York brewer who had supplied both sides with beer during the Revolutionary War, settled in the town and opened a brewhouse.

The brewhouse was acquired in 1836 by a Quaker, George Robinson, who ran it for 20 years, rebuilding the brewery and its maltings. In 1856 Robert Evans and James Phipps bought the brewery. Cornelius Evans, Robert's son, joined the business in 1865, and took command in 1873, together with two partners, James Gaul and J.H. Phipps, son of James Phipps. Evans acquired complete control of the brewery in 1878, by which time it was employing 50 men in Hudson.

The brewery's products were all in the British tradition, and its specialties were India Pale Ale and Hudson Cream Ale. It opened a bottling plant in 1889, and bottled beers became the largest part of its business. In the first decade of the twentieth century the brewery was producing 60,000 barrels of beer a year. When Prohibition came, the company tried to keep going by producing 'Checona non-intoxicating ale,' but lack of sales meant the brewery closed in 1924. It burnt down in 1929, but the brand was kept going after Prohibition ended by the Peter Barmann brewery in Kingston, New York.

Evans's rival in Hudson was Granger and Gregg, which was started in 1858 by Benjamin Millard and Stephen B. Barnard. Ezra Waterbury bought out Barnard's interest in 1864 and Millard's share in 1873. The next year he took a partner, a Mr Peabody, and Peabody was the sole proprietor from 1880 to 1881. That year the brewery was purchased by William Granger, former manager of the Albany Brewing Company, and Henry L. Gregg. By 1895 it was producing 50,000 barrels a year, when the name was changed to the Granger Brewing Company. Granger, unlike Evans, brewed lager beer, and its use of glass-lined steel tanks for lagering led it to be described as the most modern brewery in the state in 1899.

The company ceased trading in 1903, and the brewery was briefly run by the Yuengling family. In 1905 it was in the possession of the Hudson City Brewing Company, a concern that lasted only two years.

**Left** A rare tap knob bearing Evans's attractive script.

**Right** This button shows William Granger as chief of the Hudson Fire Department.

**Left and below** Table Ale was the everyday lunch or supper drink at home; an Evans ale glass

**Above** Reverse-on-glass signs, one from around 1890, the other from around 1910.

**Below** A factory scene lithograph from around 1880, before the brewery had started brewing lagers.

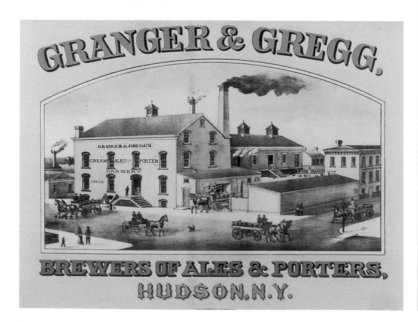

**Above** A hanging salon sign for Granger & Gregg's version of IPA.

## JW GREEN OF LUTON

Single-brewery collections rely on the brewery in question producing a quantity of good-quality memorabilia. JW Green, for many years the biggest brewery in Bedfordshire, England, and one remembered fondly for its beers by many American servicemen stationed in the area during World War II, meets all the requirements.

John William Green was only 24 when he bought Pearman's Phoenix brewery in Park Street West, Luton, in 1869. He had been working there for four years, after an initial apprenticeship with a hat manufacturer (Luton was once famous for hat making).

The Phoenix brewery's first takeover came in 1875, when Green acquired another small Luton brewer, Wadworth and Thare of Market Hill. The boost to business this brought meant that expansion of the brewery was soon required. In April 1876 the *Brewers' Guardian* announced: 'Mr JW Green of the Phoenix Brewery, Luton has entrusted Mr Kinder [a well-known Victorian brewery architect] with the enlargement of his brewery from seven to 15 quarters,' that is, from around 35 barrels of beer from each brew to a capacity of 75 barrels a time.

The Phoenix brewery's big rival in Luton was Sworder's brewery, and for many years the two fought for supremacy. Eventually Sworder's came close to bankruptcy, and in May 1897 it was put up for auction. After a spirited battle in the auction-room, the eventual buyer turned out to be JW Green himself, who paid the then staggering sum of £139,000 (around $21,000) for the brewery and its 58 tied hotels, pubs, and beerhouses.

By 1900 the Phoenix brewery had been rebuilt (by Adlams of Bristol, another well-known firm of brewery architects) to cope with the increased business the takeover of Sworder's had brought. The brewery now had 40 horses to pull the drays, and the men, who started work at 6.30 a.m., were allowed six free pints of beer a day. They were expected to wear the red stocking cap traditional to brewers, though in most other breweries this was already a dying fashion.

After World War I Green's began expanding further afield, taking over little family breweries in the surrounding market-towns of south Bedfordshire and

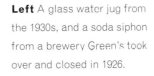

**Above** A wooden sign made by a company called Tuchfarher for Evans' India Pale Ale.

**Left** A glass water jug from the 1930s, and a soda siphon from a brewery Green's took over and closed in 1926.

east Hertfordshire. Its real expansion came after World War II, however, when the company made a dash for national status. In the five years from 1948 to the end of 1952 the Luton brewery took over seven other breweries from Sunderland in the northeast of England to Sussex in the southeast, and tripled in size to

owning just over 1,000 pubs. The managing director, Bernard Dixon, believed there would only be a dozen big breweries in Britain in a few years, and he wanted the Luton concern to be one of them. But Dixon's ambitions to turn Green's into a leading national brewer needed something he had not yet been able to find – a brand, an image, that would put it alongside the likes of the big boys, Bass and Watney. The chance came early in 1954 when Flower and Sons of Stratford-upon-Avon agreed to sell out to the Luton brewery.

Flower's was a much better-known brand name than Green's, and so the new, enlarged concern took the name of the smaller partner. However, Flower's dash for growth had run out of steam by the 1960s, and in 1962 the company was acquired by the big London brewery of Whitbread and Co. The Park Street West brewery closed in 1969.

**Above** 'That's another fine tray you've got us for the collection.' An elderly Oliver and Hardy, the great comedians and movie stars, behind the bar in a Green's pub one Christmas in the early 1950s.

**Right** A 'label' ashtray from the early 1950s.

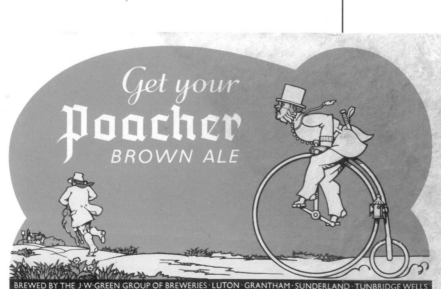

**Left** A cardboard bar ad. sign from the early 1950s.

**Above left** A cellar thermometer issued by Green's to its pub landlords, probably in the 1930s, showing the correct temperature – 55 degrees Fahrenheit – for draft cask-conditioned beer if it is not to spoil.

**Above right** Two Green's labels from around World War 2.

**Below** An Edwardian match holder advertising Green's ales on one side, and its 'table waters,' or soft drinks, on the other.

## WHITE SHIELD

For a beer brand to attract specialist collectors, it has to have history, a little romance, and, most importantly, it must generate lots of memorabilia. Worthington's White Shield has all that: it is the only surviving naturally conditioned bottled India Pale Ale with roots in the nineteenth century. The distinctive label has been seen on everything from china plant pots to transport. The White Shield car, with its bottle-shaped chassis, first appeared before World War I, and an example is now in the National Motor Museum in Beaulieu, Hampshire, England.

William Worthington began working as a cooper in Burton-upon-Trent in 1744, and bought his first brewery in 1760. At that time the Burton brewers' main trade was in strong, sweet ales sold to drinkers in Russia, Poland, and other countries around the Baltic Sea. By the 1820s this market was effectively finished, and the Burton breweries turned to paler, heavily hopped ales sold to Britons living in India – India Pale Ale, or IPA.

Worthington was one of the leaders of the trade, and when IPAs became popular in Britain its own version had a high reputation. Soon after the company merged with Bass in 1927 a chilled, pasteurized version of the beer came out which was known as Green Shield, while the original unpasteurized, unfiltered beer continued as White Shield, the shield and dagger being Worthington's trademark. White Shield was always sought out by drinkers who regarded themselves as connoisseurs. Because it was a naturally conditioned bottled beer, it contained yeast sediment. So serving White Shield required a steady hand from the bar staff in order to achieve a clear and sparkling glassful of beer, with the sediment left behind in the bottle.

Today the beer is no longer brewed at Burton, but by the small Sussex brewery of King and Barnes. The modern label is a clear descendant of the original glorious red, black, and white label that has graced bottles since at least the end of the nineteenth century, though the wording on the scroll above the shield has changed from 'India Pale Ale' through 'Original Pale Ale,' and, today, it is 'White Shield.'

**Right** A brass bottle opener shaped like the beer label from the early 1990s.

# Specialist collections

**Above** This gorgeous ceramic water jug, its lines so very clearly those of the early 1930s, bears the brewer's name in a typeface that also appeared on contemporary advertising.

**Above** A 1960 coaster advertising Worthington White Shield.

**Below** The cover of a booklet of limericks issued to advertise the brand in the 1930s.

**Above** A 'label' ashtray from the early 1950s.

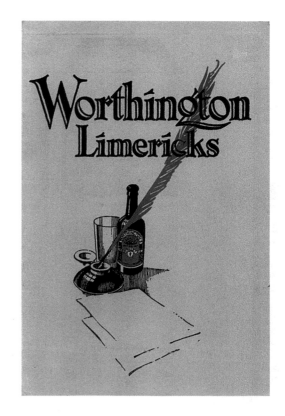

**Above** Not a bottle, but a bottle-shaped advertising flyer.

**Left** A lovely white match holder from around the time of World War I.

# RESOURCES

## COLLECTIBLES WEB SITES

The best place for finding beer memorabilia is on the web where auction sites, such as www.e-bay.com can throw up more than 9,000 items covering every kind of breweriana you could imagine. Specific sites dedicated to beer memorabilia include:

**American Breweriana Association**
www.a-b-a.com *Great pictures of assorted beer memorabilia, lots of links to collectors' own sites, other beer sites and so on. Irritating music.*

**American Museum of Brewing History and Arts** oldenberg.com/oldenberg/museum.html *The Kentucky-based AMBHA's own site.*

**Association of Bottled Beer Collectors**
www.ourworld.compuserve.com/homepages/johnmann/abbchome.htm *Home site of the British ABBC: links to other British beer site.*

**Beer Can Collectors of America**
www.bcca.com/index.html *Cans, cans, cans.*

**The Beer Cap Page** www.cam.org/~kibi/tbcp *Exactly what it says: plenty of information about collecting crown corks, links to commercial and private sites, screen savers, tips and news.*

**Beer History** www.beerhistory.com *Pictures, information, on-line resources and book sales on the history of beer.*

**BrewerianaNet** www.craftbrewers.com/breweriananet/index.shtml *Free classified ads for memorabilia collectors, index of collectors.*

**CELCE (Spanish collectors' club)**
www.uv.es/~avalino/celce.htm

**Federation of Historic Bottle Collectors**
www.fohbc.com

**Museum of Beverage Containers and Advertising** www.gono.com/museum/ *Virtual museum tours.*

## COLLECTORS' WEB SITES

www.oldbeerstuff.com *Ruddy Lechler's Stegmeier-oriented site: see one man's obsession with one brewery.*

www.juni.com.pl/~beerlabel/labels.html *An excellent site run by Polish collector Radoslav Kwiecien.*

beercoasters.silesianet.pl *Another good Polish site, this one dedicated to coasters.*

website.lineone.net/~tonypeach/index.html *British coaster collector Tony Peach's well-designed beer mats and coasters pages.*

www.angelfire.com/mo/trayman/ *More trays than you have ever seen.*

labolog.zero.cz/ *A bottle label site from the Czech Republic.*

www.geocities.com/eureka/3518 *Venezuelan beer can collector Marcello Gagliardi's pages.*

## WHERE TO SEE MEMORABILIA

### EUROPE

**Belgium**
**Confederation of Belgian Brewers Museum,** Brewers' House Grand'Place 10, 1000 Brussels Tel: 2 511 49 87 Open daily 10 to 5.

**Gambrinus Drivers Museum,** 2 Avenue Fontaine St Pierre, B5600 Romedenne (Philippeville) Tel/Fax 32 82 67 83 48 *Claims to be the only museum in the world dedicated to brewery delivery trucks. Also has a collection of beer memorabilia.*

**Czech Republic**
**Pivovarske Museum,** Veleslavinova 6, 301 14 Plzen (Pilsen) Tel: 19 733 4955/723 5574 *Owned by the Pilsner Urquell brewery in Pilsen. Open daily 10 to 6.*

**Denmark**
**Carlsberg Visitors' Centre,** Gamle Carlsberg Vej 11 2500 Valby. *Open Monday to Friday, 10 to 4.*

**France**
**Musée Européen de la Bière,** Rue de la Citadelle - BP 17 F-55700 Stenay, Lorraine Tel: 3 29 80 68 78; e-mail: stenay@mygale.org; www.mygale.org/09/stenay *Open March 1 to November 30, 10-12 and 2-6 General museum of brewing with fine section on beer memorabilia, including posters, ashtrays, bottles, glasses and the rest.*

**Musée Français de la Brasserie,** 62 rue Charles Courtois F-54210 Saint-Nicholas-de-Port, Lorraine Tel 83 46 95 52 *In the old Vézelize brewery. A good selection of odd beer memorabilia, as well as some beautiful old posters. The building is now a national monument.*

**Great Britain**
**Bass Museum,** Horninglow Street, Burton upon Trent, Staffordshire DE14 1YQ Tel: 1283 511000; Fax: 1283 513509; e-mail: bookings@museum.brewers.bass.co.uk *An excellent and family-friendly museum. Pre-booked brewery tours, which include admission to the museum and a meal.*

**John Smith's Brewery,** Tadcaster, North Yorkshire LS24 9SA Tel: 1937 837421 *Brewing memorabilia on view in the archives room. Telephone to book.*

**Fuller, Smith and Turner, Griffin Brewery,** Chiswick Lane South, Chiswick, London W4 2QB Tel: 181 996 2000 *Brewery tours take place four times a day on Mondays, Wednesdays, Thursdays and Fridays: pre-booking is essential. Tours take in the whole brewing process, passing through the Hock Cellar, where the company displays old posters, bottles, photographs and the like.*

**Ireland**
**Guinness Hop Store Visitors' Centre,** Crane Street, St James' Gate, Dublin 8 Tel: (1) 408 4800 *Seasonal opening times. Check beforehand. Admission includes free drink in Hop Store bar. Attractions include the Advertising Gallery, the muesum, an audio-visual show and a souvenir shop with the world's greatest selection of Guinness memorabilia.*

**The Netherlands**
**Bier Reclame Museum,** Haagweg 375 4813 XC, Breda Tel: 76 522 09 75 *Open Sundays 11 to 11. More than 950 enamel beer advertising signs and thousands of other beer memorabilia items. Has a beer café.*

### AMERICA

**American Museum of Brewing History and Arts,** Oldenberg Brewing Co, 400 Buttermilk Pike, Ft Mitchell, Kentucky 41017 Tel: 606-341 7223 *Open 10-5. Entry includes tasting. Claims to have the widest range of brewery collectibles in the world.*

**Museum of Beverage Containers and Advertising,** 1055 Ridgecrest Drive, Millersville, Tennessee 37072 Tel: 615 859 5236 ext 218 or 1-877 826 4929 *Open 9 to 5 Monday to Saturday, 1 to 5 Sunday.*

## MEMORABILIA SOCIETIES

### AMERICA

**Argentina**
**Circulo Argentino de Coleccionismo Cervecero,** c/o Dr.Daniel P. Quintana Uruguay 390 Piso 16 o, f.252 (1015) Buenos Aires

**Asociacion Argentina de Coleccionismo e Intercambio Cervecero**
c/o Dr.Juan Carlos De Marco Calle 50 Num.735 (1900) La Plata

**Canada**
**British Columbia Breweriana Collectors,** c/o Larry Sampson, 259 Watling Street, Burnaby, British Columbia, V5J 1V4

**The Canadian Brewerianist,** c/o Andy Reiner, 19 Lambert Road, Thornhill, Ontario

**United States of America**
**American Breweriana Association,** PO Box 11157, Pueblo, Colorado 81001-0157 *52-page bi-monthly magazine.*

**Beer Can Collectors of America,** 747 Merus Court, Fenton, Missouri 63026-2092 *Bimonthly Beercans and Brewery Collectibles.*

**Crown Cap Collectors Society International,** John Vetter, 4300 San Juan Drive, Fairfax, Virginia 22030

**East Coast Breweriana Association (ECBA)** c/o John Stanley, 3712 Sunningdale Way, Durham, North Carolina 27707-5684

**Federation of Historical Bottle Collectors,** 88 Sweetbriar Branch, Longwood, Florida 32750-2783

**Microbes (ECBA/NABA micro-breweries chapter),** c/o Chris and Roger Levesque. PO Box 826, South Windsor, Connecticut 06074-0826

**National Association Brewery Advertising (NABA),** 2343 Met-to Wee-Lane, Wauwatosa, Wisconsin 53226 *Quarterly journal The Breweriana Collector.*

## EUROPE

**Austria**
**Erster Osterreichisher Brauerei-Sammler-Club,** Johann Sochatzy, Breitwiesergutstrasse 46, A-4020 Linz

**Belgium**
**Gambrinus Club van Belgie,** Brusselsesteenweg, 47 B-3080 Tervuren

**Les Amis du Verre Bier et des Brasseries Anciennes,** 18, rue de Moulin, B-7032 Spiennes

**Selecta Antwerp Club Collecting Brewery,** c/o Van de Vloed Marcel, Van Reethstraat 19, 2170 Merksem

**Czech Republic**
**Klub Sberatelu Brno,** Kroftova 66 602 00 Brno

**Labolog,** P.O.Box 24 400 10 Usti Nad Labem

**Denmark**
**FORT Samlerforeningen,** Tarnvej 159,2 DK-2610 Rodovre,

**Skandinavisk Bryggerisouvenir Samlerforening,** c/o Flemming S. Pedersen, Bryggervangen 4, 3th DK-2100 Copenhagen

**Estonia**
**Club Baltic,** P.O. Box 2086, EE-0029 Tallin

**France**
**Association Bourbonnaise des Collectionneurs d'articles publicitaires de brasserie anciennes et modernes,** 33 Bel Air, F-03000 Neuvy

**Brassicol,** 2, Rue Moll, F-67000 Strasbourg

**Gambrinus France,** 18, Avenue de Lattre de Tassigny, F-92360 Meudon, La Foret

**Germany**
**Fördergemeinschaft von Brauerei Werbemittel Sammlern,** Sylviastrasse 16 D-45131 Essen

**German Breweriana Collector Society,** Hon Treasurer Martin Apeler, Brinkstrasse 52 D-31840 Hess.Oldendorf

**Internationaler Brauerei-kultur-Verband (IBV),** Winfried Friedel, IBV-ZentralePostfach 30 04 05 D-70444 Stuttgart *Membership secretary:* Ingrid Stossberger, Pfarrwiesenallee 27, D-71067 Sindelfingen *Special interest sections of the IBV Coasters/beer mats:* Gunther Maldaner, Max-Planck-Ring 3, D-40764 Langenfeld *Labels:* Markus Hillenbrand, Wiesenweg 7, D-69168 Wiesloch-Baiertal *Beer glasses:* Eberhard Ziebarth, Blocksberg 3, D-21465 Reinbek

*Crown corks:* Walter Lachmund, Martinstrasse 10, D-12167 Berlin

**Great Britain**
**Association of Bottled Beer Collectors,** Graham Tubb, 66 High Street, Puckeridge, Ware, Herts SG11 1RX

**British Beercan Collectors' Society,** Roger Tucker, 22 Hill Close, Plympton, Plymouth, Devon PL7 1QG

**British Beermat Collectors Society,** Tony Matthews, 69 Dunnington Avenue, Kidderminster, Worcestershire DY10 2YT

**British Brewery Playing Card Society,** Maxine Chantry, 42 Booth Way Little Paxton, St Neots, Cambridgeshire PE19 4PT

**Labologists' Society,** Jim Gartside (membership secretary), 52 Grove Avenue, London W7 3ES

**Brewery History Society,** Jeff Sechiari, Manor Side East, Mill Lane, Byfleet, West Byfleet, Surrey KT14 7RS

**Italy**
**Amici della Birra,** Via Ciri, 46 I10077 San Maurizio Canavese

**Art Collection,** c/o Sergio Mazzolenavia, via L. da Vinci 35 I-03043 Cassino

**Il Barattolo,** Casella Postale 268 I-20101 Milan

**The Netherlands**
**Blik Op Blik,** c/o Henk Hensttav "Blik Op Blik" Ambachtslaan 21 NL-5506 AD Veldhoven

**Brouwery-Artikelen Verzamelaars,** Spreenwenlaan 31 NL-2566 ZM Den Haag

**Norway**
**International Beer Club**
Postboks 35 4993 Sundebru

**Poland**
**Bielski Klub Kolekcjonerow,** Ul. Spoldzielcow 18-42 PL-43 300 Bielsko Biala

**Slovakia**
**Danubius Club,** Cintorinska, 32 811 08 Bratislava

**Spain**
**CELCE,** Colon, 9 E-46004 Valencia

**Sweden**
**Bryggeryklubben,** Runvgen 6 S-13755 Vesterhaninge

**Switzerland**
**Gambrinus Tauschring der Schweizer Bierteller-Sammler,** Postfach 304 CH-9001 St Gallen

## AFRICA

**Zimbabwe/South Africa**
**African Breweriana Society,** Peter Gorman, c/o Manica Air Cargo PO Box AP5 Harare Airport

## ASIA

**China**
**Chinese Label Collectors,** Rm 201, Unit 1, Bldg 12/South Laodong Resid. Quarters Changhzhou, Jangsu 213001

## AUSTRALASIA

**Australia**
**Australian Beer Can Collectors Society,** 20 Seymour Terrace Ascot Park South Australia 5043

**National Beer Can Collectors Inc,** 34 Bulgin Avenue Wynnum, West Queensland 4178

**Victoria Beer Label Collectors' Society,** George Crompton (Secretary), 11 Dublin Avenue, Strathmore 3041, Victoria

**New Zealand**
**New Zealand Beer Can Collectors Society,** c/o Brian Collinge, 66 Dehli Crescent Khandallah Wellington

**North of the Bombays,** c/o Ken Ayton, 96 Weldene Street Glenfield Auckland

# INDEX